AF778791

How to $ave 25% Plu$ on Your Auto In$urance

The Book Your Agent Doesn't Want You to Read!

By Alan Abler

Copyright © 1997 by Alan Abler, All rights reserved.

The text of this publication, or any part thereof, may not be reproduced in any manner without expressed, written permission of the publisher and author.

Published by Heidi House LTD
For mail orders, write: Heidi House LTD, 18631 N. 19th Avenue, Suite #128-222, Phoenix, Arizona 85027 or call 1-888-511-6070 or visit us on the net at http://www.heidihouse.com/book.

Reasonable care has been taken in the preparation of this book to ensure accuracy. This book is sold with the understanding that the author and publisher are not rendering legal or other professional services. Laws vary from state to state, and readers with specific questions should seek the professional services of an advisor in their area.

The author and publisher specifically disclaim directly or indirectly, any liability, loss or risk, personal or otherwise, which is incurred as a result of the use and application of any information in this book.

Table of Contents

Dedication

This book is dedicated to the many loyal customers I've had the pleasure of doing business with over the past years, many of whom were with me for over 20 years. I would like to say ***"thank you."*** This book is also dedicated to the many people I've worked with during my career who have contributed to my overall views, perceptions and knowledge of the industry. Without their unknowing help, this book could not have been written. To all I say ***"thank you."***

Introduction

After 20+ years in the insurance industry, I realized many things could have been improved but were not. I was especially dissatisfied with the way the public was perceiving the issue of their auto insurance. They were basing their auto insurance coverages, choices and decisions, solely on the way the insurance industry had trained them to do, or by asking the agent, "What does the average person do?" They seldom made decisions for themselves as to what course of action was best for their situation.

I was amazed at how willing they were to believe anything their agent or company representative told them, never looking at the policy for themselves. I realize that in the past, policies were written in such a way that even I, an insurance agent, couldn't understand them, let alone my customers. It is therefore reasonable to assume that my customers were not in the habit of looking at their policies, but in the habit of calling me. This has changed in the last few years. The policies are now written so the average person can read and understand them. Most of the legalese has been rewritten into everyday language.

In real estate the three most important words are location, location, location; in auto insurance the three most important words are ***simple, simple, simple!***

We have lost our focus, drifting away from the original purpose for auto insurance. Auto insurance was conceived with the idea of pooling small amounts of capital with others, having the funds necessary if any member of the group had an accident and could not afford to pay for the loss on his own! ***Today, it's big business with the industry in a tireless endeavor to get your money!*** They want you to insure for any and everything imaginable, regardless of whether you could self insure that item or not! ***It's time for the consumer to "wake up" and take control of their insurance affairs!***

With all the changes taking place in the insurance industry, as well as changes in technology, it is becoming increasingly clear that the days of the auto insurance agent are numbered. The fact is, you, the insurance consumer, has the ability to handle your own auto insurance needs without the help of an agent. In searching for books on this subject, I found nothing that gave an in-depth look at the subject and encouraged or adequately equipped you to handle your auto insurance, ***putting the savings in your pocket!*** In realizing this, I saw a need for such a book. Hopefully, this book will not only help you understand all the aspects of your auto insurance, but also help you ***save 25% plus*** on your auto insurance premium in the process, for many years to come!

In this book you will learn the basic coverages available in an auto policy and the information needed to make intelligent choices for tailoring your auto policy. Chapter 1 is the most important of all chapters. It is foundational to becoming your own auto insurance agent.

In Chapter 2 you will be informed of the valuable resources that are found in your state department of insurance. Many people don't realize the wealth of information that is available to the insurance consumer from the state department of insurance.

Chapter 3 deals with selecting an insurance company, and if you still feel a need for one, an agent. This chapter is full of valuable information that to my knowledge has never been put together in a simple format and made available to the public. Once you digest the information in this chapter, you will become skillful in selecting an insurance company. You will also have a good understanding of how the insurance company views you, the insurance consumer.

Chapter 4 takes an in-depth look at the claims process. With the information in this chapter, you will never again be on the short end of the stick when settling a claim.

Finally, in Chapter 5, we will take a glimpse into the future. Please realize I don't have a crystal ball, but there are changes taking place in the insurance industry that any thinking person would come to similar conclusions. The handwriting is on the wall, figuratively speaking. The changes coming are in line with the rest of our world; major, innovative and profitable to the astute. Realizing what is ahead will not only prepare you for the changes, but put you on the cutting edge by knowing what to look for and what to watch out for. You will be ahead of the pack and profit from it!

I realize that the information in this book has the potential of putting many agents out of good paying jobs, but they must realize it's coming and may as well be prepared. ***You, the insurance buying public, can profit from these changes.*** Hopefully, this book will speed up the process. There may be more details in this book than necessary but hang in there, I want to paint a complete word picture of the state of affairs to enable you to see the big picture and realize the importance of why I've written in such detail.

In the back of this book is information on obtaining a guide for homeowner's, renter's and condominium owner's insurance. This is written as a supplement to the auto book since a great deal of the information in this book you are about to read would be duplicated if I were to write a complete book on each of the above subjects. The chapters dealing with company selection and the state department of insurance would be duplicates of what has been written in this book.

Also available in the back of this book is information on obtaining a guide on the simple subject of life insurance. The insurance and financial planning industries have made life insurance out to be a complex subject, but in reality it's not! ***"The Great Life Insurance Hoax"*** exposes the way the life insurance industry has taken advantage of you and me over the years. They have told us that we need life insurance in more ways and in greater amounts than is really necessary! They have built in for themselves a guaranteed profit at our expense! ***You won't want to miss this important money saving book!***

If you do all, or even a portion of what is outlined, you will be on the road to ***saving 25% plus on your auto insurance! Enjoy the book!***

Chapter 1

Auto Insurance Coverages

Chapter 1

Auto Insurance Coverages

1. Liability Coverage

This coverage is without a doubt the most important coverage of the auto insurance policy! In my 20 plus years as an insurance agent, I have encountered many people who have assets to protect but don't have a clue as to how to properly protect those assets. I'm referring to home and business owners who carry state minimum liability coverage on their vehicles thinking they are not taking unwarranted risks. They share a common attitude that they are careful drivers and an accident won't happen to them. However, I have seen it happen. None of us are immune to making an error in judgment or having a mechanical breakdown that causes an accident. I have seen it happen time and time again!

Liability coverage, which includes bodily injury and property damage, is one of the most expensive and least understood coverages of the auto insurance policy. An understanding of this coverage is essential in evaluating your insurance needs in this area so you don't over or under insure, the latter being the most common.

How Liability Coverage Works

To begin with there are two parts to your liability coverage. The first is bodily injury liability coverage. Bodily injury liability coverage is simple to understand, contrary to the belief of the general public. It protects you against liability that you would incur if you were the cause of an accident which resulted in injuries to another party.

The person(s) injured may be in another vehicle, a pedestrian or a passenger in your vehicle. This does not normally include another named insured on your policy, such as your spouse. You cannot be libel to yourself. You need to check with your insurance company for a definition of a named insured as they define it in your policy. This could vary from company to company and state to state, depending on the laws governing insurance in your state.

There are many areas covered under bodily injury liability coverage that most people are not aware of; however, bodily injury liability coverage is very basic once you grasp the concept.

The first and most obvious is medical expenses incurred by the person(s) injured. However, that is just the beginning of covered expenses. You are also libel for their time off work and other actual expenses incurred, such as mileage to and from the doctor, medication, and of course, let's not forget pain and suffering, which is one of the most abused provisions in the entire coverage! People sometimes forget when they have been involved in an auto accident and are filing their claim that they have not won the lottery.

In more serious cases of death, or long- or short-term disability, your bodily injury liability coverage includes the costs incurred by the fault free party for these expenses. This includes replacement of lost income to a family whose breadwinner dies or is disabled and unable to produce income for the family. While it is hard to calculate the financial loss of a family member, bodily injury liability coverage protects you from being personally responsible to the party or parties that were injured in the accident.

The second coverage in the liability category is property damage. Property damage liability covers you against loss for any property which is damaged as a result of an accident, excluding your vehicle. Many insurance consumers don't realize that property damage liability is not just limited to hitting another motorist's vehicle. Have you ever seen a car wrapped around a utility pole or inside a building?

Many people are only interested in carrying the minimum liability coverage required by state law. They fail to stop and think that the average car today costs about $20,000, with many cars costing in excess of $25,000. They don't realize that they would be personally responsible for any and all costs associated with the repair or replacement of a vehicle they damage in excess of their property damage liability coverage; not to mention the costs involved if they were responsible for a multi-car accident.

When you understand the personal risks involved by carrying lower liability limits, you soon realize that the small additional cost to increase property damage liability is worth doing. I have seen numerous cases over the years where the "at fault" party was paying back a property damage claim to the insurance company on a monthly basis until the entire amount was repaid! This is the result of carrying inadequate property damage liability coverage. It is my personal belief that $100,000 property damage liability should be the minimum amount of coverage carried.

Did you know that you could be held responsible for an accident, never having touched another vehicle? An example of this is when you cause another motorist to hit a vehicle or object or even leave the road altogether, to avoid being hit by you. This could result not only in a property damage liability claim but also in a bodily injury liability claim as discussed earlier.

Do you realize the potential cost of a utility pole? We are talking about more than just the cost to replace the pole. You could also be responsible to the utility company for lost revenue because of the power outage to its customers. The total cost of hitting a utility pole could easily run into thousands of dollars.

What about the cost of hitting a building? If it's a commercial building you not only have the cost of repairing the building but also lost revenue to the businesses while repairs are being made plus other miscellaneous expenses. Even though the owner of the building may have insurance to cover the damage, their insurance company will look to you for reimbursement. This is called subrogation. Reimbursement to the insurance company can be made by writing a check, utilizing your property damage liability coverage, or paying on a monthly installment plan. The insurance company could even garnish your wages if they chose to!

Now that we have an overview of how bodily injury liability and property damage liability coverages work, I would like you to ask yourself the question, ***"What coverages are right for me?"***

Many people, when shopping for auto insurance, are clueless as to what coverages and limits they should have. Naturally, they are looking for the lowest price or the minimum coverages allowable by state law. They seldom do a proper evaluation as to what coverages and limits are right for them.

Let's look at bodily injury liability coverage and gain an understanding of how low the minimum limits are that the state requires. I realize these limits may vary from state to state, but a standard minimum coverage is $15,000 per person and $30,000 per accident for bodily injury liability. This means if you are responsible for the injury, death or disability of another person, $15,000 is the maximum coverage you have for one person and no more than $30,000 if two or more people are injured in the accident. In essence, if 2 or 20 people are injured in the accident, you only have a total of $30,000 coverage. It doesn't take a rocket scientist to realize that carrying low limits of bodily injury liability coverage is trouble looking for a place to happen!

Think of it this way. If you were the person injured or disabled, or you lost a member of your family, how much coverage would you want the person responsible for the accident to have? ***This is a good starting point for you to consider how much bodily injury liability coverage is right for you.***

Another way of looking at it is how do you feel about moral obligation to your fellow man? I would like to think that if I made an error in driving or had a mechanical failure of my vehicle that resulted in an accident, I would be able to restore, at least financially, what I took away from someone else. This in my opinion is the most important consideration.

Another important aspect to consider is what do I have to protect. Over the years many people have said to me, "I don't have anything to lose" or "I have assets

I need to protect." What the "nothing to lose" group fails to realize is that while they may not have money in the bank, property or other assets, they have an ability to produce income that could be attached if they lost a lawsuit. This fallacy is common among students and young people who may appear to have the least to lose now, but because of their age, have the most to lose in future earning power. Many times they mistakenly take that risk.

The "I have assets to protect" group often chooses the maximum coverage they can buy. This usually means $100,000 per person, $300,000 per accident for bodily injury liability, and $100,000 property damage liability. Many times they also opt for an excess or umbrella policy that gives an additional $1 million to $5 million of liability protection.

It is my opinion that $100,000 per person, $300,000 per accident bodily injury liability and $100,000 property damage liability along with an excess or umbrella policy for $1 million, should be strongly considered for the reasons mentioned above.

There are other limits of coverage for bodily injury liability that range between $15,000 per person, $30,000 per accident, and the $100,000 per person, $300,000 per accident. If you feel that somewhere in the middle is best for you, you can select from various coverage combinations. Some insurance companies offer bodily injury limits of $250,000 per person, $500,000 per accident. However, you may be able to buy a $1 million excess or umbrella policy for little more than the difference in premium and have a lot more protection for the money.

You need to evaluate your affordability level, your personal feelings about moral obligation, as well as protecting what is yours now and in the future. ***It's your decision!***

2. Uninsured and Underinsured Motorist Coverages

These coverages protect you and your passengers from the financial loss incurred due to an accident caused by a driver who has no insurance or insufficient amounts of insurance. Contrary to popular belief, these coverages do not cover the other driver. ***You are protecting yourself!*** Another major misunderstanding about these coverages is they do not cover your vehicle for physical damage. Check with your insurance company to see if the collision coverage on your policy would cover you in such an event, or if additional material damage coverage is needed to cover your vehicle. If your collision coverage covers your vehicle, you may want to purchase a collision deductible waiver (if available), to ease your concerns about paying your deductible in such an occurrence.

Policies vary from state to state but in most cases uninsured and underinsured motorist coverages cover you in any motor vehicle you are in, as well as being a pedestrian or riding a bicycle. These coverages act as the other person's bodily injury liability since they didn't carry adequate coverage. In other words, your insurance company is now liable to cover your medical expenses, time off from work, pain and suffering, death, disability or other miscellaneous related expenses.

State requirements may vary from a minimum of $15,000 per person, $30,000 per accident, to no requirement for these coverages at all. The limits of uninsured and underinsured motorist coverages selected guarantee you the minimum amount of protection you will have in the event of another driver's error or negligence.

At this point, I would like to briefly address "no fault" coverage. Some states are "no fault states" which means, by law, your coverage is different than I have outlined above. In these states, you select the amount of bodily injury protection you desire and purchase that coverage from your insurance carrier. Each state's laws vary, making it almost impossible to cover this topic in detail. However, I will say this, you have to use the same considerations in selecting "no fault" coverage as you do in selecting your uninsured and underinsured motorist coverages as I have outlined.

One of the most frequent and expensive mistakes people make is duplicating coverages. What I mean by this is they carry coverages on their auto policy that they are already covered for on other policies. The only area of coverage not duplicated by another policy, and can only be covered by the auto policy, is coverage for pain and suffering.

Examples of duplicated coverages that may exist under uninsured and underinsured motorist coverages are as follows:

You may be carrying major medical coverage for you and your family with a $500 deductible and a co-pay of 20% up to a limit of $1,500 out of pocket per person, with a maximum out of pocket of $4,500 per family. You may also be carrying life insurance on yourself and your spouse and possibly disability insurance through your employer. In addition, social security has survivor benefits for dependent children under the age of 18 if the parent dies and is covered by social security. There are also disability benefits for the worker covered under social security.

The next step is to check with your major medical, life and disability insurance companies to see what coverages you already have so you can determine what limits of uninsured and underinsured motorist coverages you need. You don't want to purchase duplicate coverages from your auto insurance carrier; that's throwing money away since most policies will not make duplicate payments. Duplicate payments will be discussed in more detail a little later.

Unlike liability coverage where your risk in theory is unlimited, here we can evaluate our needs based on the coverages you already have. Here are several questions you should ask yourself. How much risk do I have before my medical coverage pays 100%? Is my life insurance adequate? If not, in most cases it is better to upgrade the life insurance since you are not limited to coverage only in the event of an auto accident. What about disability coverage? This is often the most neglected of all non-auto coverages.

My personal opinion on uninsured and underinsured motorist coverages is as follows: You need to evaluate the cost of uninsured and underinsured motorist coverages at minimum limits and higher limits and then decide if the extra cost is worth it. Look at the cost of $15,000 per person, $30,000 per accident, versus the next several levels, say $25,000 per person, $50,000 per accident, $50,000 per person, $100,000 per accident or $100,000 per person, $300,000 per accident. You may notice that going from the minimum limits to the next level is fairly reasonable in price while going to the higher limits could become a bit pricey.

If the state in which you live has no requirement for uninsured or underinsured motorist coverages, it's your decision whether you carry the coverages at all. I hope I have given you the tools necessary to make an educated evaluation and decision for yourself.

3. Medical Coverage

Most auto policies with medical coverage will pay medical expenses for an injury resulting from an automobile accident regardless of who is at fault. Injuries as simple as slamming your thumb in the car door to being seriously injured in an auto accident are covered. You would be covered even if you are injured while getting in or out of a vehicle.

It's important to know which type of medical coverage you have on your auto policy. Some policies pay regardless of any other medical coverage you carry while other policies cover only as "excess medical." In essence, they pay only after you have exhausted your major medical coverage, the uninsured and/or underinsured motorist coverages, or the other person's bodily injury liability. Usually, if the medical coverage is "excess medical," the premium will be substantially lower than medical coverage that pays no matter what other medical coverages you may have. Some companies offer auto medical coverage with a deductible at a slightly lower rate. That leads to the next consideration. ***Do you need auto medical coverage?***

Here are some thoughts to consider in making your evaluation regarding this coverage. The first and most important question to ask yourself, "Do I have major medical coverage?" If the answer is yes, review your policy to determine what your maximum out of pocket risk is after your deductibles and co-payments are met. An excellent way to do this is to call your major medical benefits department and ask these questions. "If I'm involved in an auto accident and injured and have no other coverage to pay my medical expenses, how does my plan work? What is my maximum out of pocket expense before the plan pays 100%?" Answers to these simple questions will tell you what your maximum out of pocket risk is.

You must also remember that if the accident isn't your fault, you would have medical coverage under the other person's bodily injury liability coverage. If the other party involved had no bodily injury liability coverage or not enough coverage, your uninsured motorist or underinsured motorist coverages would pay your medical expenses up to the policy limits.

To sum it up, if the only true risk you would incur is your deductible and/or co-payment on your major medical insurance and you can afford that risk, you should ask yourself, ***"Do I need the medical coverage on my auto insurance?"*** The savings of premium dollars, ***5% to 10%,*** realized by not carrying auto medical coverage would be substantial. Remember, you have to be at fault in the accident to pay anything out of pocket if you have uninsured motorist coverage. Some people don't have the money to risk self insuring the major medical deductible and/or co-payment. If you are in that group, buy only the amount of medical coverage you need to meet those costs. Coverage is usually available in $1,000 or $5,000 increments up to $100,000. Some insurance companies include medical coverage in their policies that cannot be excluded. Bear in mind in that instance, you are paying for the coverage whether you want it or not. So evaluate your maximum risk, your ability to pay that amount, the chances of being at fault in an accident, and the cost to insure for medical coverage on your auto insurance policy. You decide what's best for you.

The major misunderstanding about auto medical coverage is, "What about my passengers?" In most states and in most policies, the passengers are covered by the "at fault" party's bodily injury liability coverage or your uninsured and/or underinsured motorist coverages. The only way you would be responsible for your passengers medical expenses is if the accident was your fault. If that were the case, your bodily injury liability would cover them. In addition, if they carry uninsured and/or underinsured motorist coverages on their own auto insurance, they would be covered to their policy limits no matter who was at fault. Their auto medical and/or major medical coverage, if carried, would also cover them.

Medical coverage is probably the most duplicated coverage in the auto policy. Most people who carry major medical coverage don't need the additional

medical coverage on their auto policy.

4. Auto Collision Coverage

Auto collision coverage covers your vehicle for damage that results from an accident. Collision damage isn't limited to driving down the road and colliding with another vehicle. If your vehicle is parked in a parking lot and damaged by another vehicle, that is also considered collision damage. Hopefully, the party at fault will be considerate enough to leave you a note with the necessary information allowing you to claim your vehicle damage on their property damage liability. If not, the damage is covered by the collision coverage on your auto policy, less your deductible.

How Collision Coverage Works

Collision coverage and claim procedures vary from company to company. It is important that you check with your current insurance company to be sure their procedures are structured to meet your needs. You may need to shop insurance companies if your current company doesn't offer what you need.

Collision claims, depending on the coverage selected, are settled in the following ways:

1. Actual cash value at time of loss. The insurance company will only pay you what your vehicle is worth on the resale market at the time of loss, less your deductible. This is assuming that your vehicle is a total loss.

2. New for old replacement. This coverage allows you to replace the vehicle with a new one of like make, model and current year. This is an option with most insurance companies and available only on new vehicles at time of purchase or lease. Depending on the insurance company selected, there may be an additional charge for this provision but it is helpful to keep you from being ***"upside down"*** on a vehicle obligation if a total loss occurs. What I mean by ***"upside down"*** is when the balance of your loan or lease obligation is higher than the value of your vehicle at time of loss. This can happen in the first three to four years after you purchase or lease a new vehicle. If that happened, you would be personally responsible for the difference unless you had new for old coverage.

What About Repairing A Vehicle?

Repairing a vehicle can be handled in several ways. The first way is to repair the vehicle with manufacturer replacement parts. This is the most expensive option for an insurance company and therefore seldom used. The most common method is to use ***"after market parts."*** After market parts are parts that have been manufactured by someone other than the original manufacturer of the vehicle. Some insurance companies even authorize the use of ***"used parts"*** to repair your vehicle.

In my view, it isn't a big deal either way as long as the work is done correctly and the used part isn't a wear part. What I mean by a wear part is a part that can wear out, such as an axle on a four wheel drive vehicle or some other mechanical part. A non-wear part such as a hood, side or quarter panel doesn't matter as much. If you live where rust is a problem, you wouldn't want used auto body parts for obvious reasons. After market parts are not a problem unless the thickness of the metal is reduced from original manufacturer's specifications. If you use a reputable body shop for the repairs, your vehicle may be rebuilt better than the original manufacturer's work.

If these issues are of concern to you, check with your current insurance company. Also when shopping for auto insurance, add this to your list of questions to ask.

Evaluate Risk Vs. Cost

A common mistake people make when buying collision coverage is an emotional one, which is also a very expensive one, and hard to convince them otherwise. Many people purchase a new vehicle and want a low collision deductible. They are emotionally attached to their purchase and feel that the lower deductible provides better protection for their investment; however, that is the opposite of correct thinking. For example: you traded in your old $5,000 vehicle and purchased a new $25,000 vehicle. On the old car you had a $250 deductible on collision coverage. Most people wouldn't think of increasing their deductible to $500 or $1,000 on the new car because they are looking at the value of what they just purchased rather than looking at their true risk, the deductible! ***Whether your vehicle is worth $5,000 or $25,000, your risk is only the deductible.***

The truth of the matter is the higher the value of the vehicle, the greater the savings by going to the higher deductible! You have to evaluate your risk (the deductible), and compare it with the savings realized by having the higher deductible. This applies not only to purchasing a new vehicle, but right now with your existing vehicle(s).

For example: you have a vehicle worth $5,000 and the cost of collision coverage with a $250 deductible is $250 per year. Raising the deductible to $500 would reduce the collision coverage cost to $175 per year. The question is this, is the $75 per year savings worth risking an additional $250? This gives you a 3.3 year break-even period, which means it will take 3.3 years to save the $250 of additional deductible risk you took by changing your collision coverage to the $500 deductible. You figure this by dividing the $75 savings realized each year, into the $250 of additional risk. What do you think your odds are of having an accident in the future? A better way to evaluate this is to ask yourself, “How many times in the last X number of years have I had to use my collision coverage and pay my deductible?” Your past experiences are an excellent guide to the future. This is one of the tools the insurance companies use to evaluate you as a risk. ***Remember, if the other party is at fault, you can claim your damage under their property damage liability assuming they have coverage.***

Now let's use the same example, only this time lets look at a more expensive vehicle, say a $40,000 vehicle. The $250 collision deductible might cost $500 per year while the $500 deductible might cost $350 per year. Now you are saving $150 and risking the same $250, which is the difference between $250 and $500 deductible, giving you a 1.67 year break-even period. At this point, you may want to consider a $1,000 collision deductible and experience additional savings. ***The ideal break-even period is 4 to 5 years, which is a statistically conservative time frame. Remember, the shorter the break-even period, the higher the incentive to raise your collision deductible.*** The savings will vary based on where you live and the rate structure for that area. The only way to know for certain is to do some shopping and get the actual numbers.

Now that you have the numbers in hand, the next thing you have to do is ask yourself the question, "If I choose the higher deductible for the savings, do I have the ability to pay the higher deductible if something happened today?" If the answer is no, you should consider keeping the lower deductible and saving the money required for the higher deductible risk. Once the money is saved and in the bank, you can then increase the deductible to a higher level where it is comfortable for you. An added bonus is the money set aside will earn interest and give you additional savings.

Another common way of thinking about deductibles is now that my vehicle is older I want to raise my collision deductible. This is not always the best thing to do at this time since the cost of collision coverage is now lower because the value of the vehicle is lower, but you are still risking the same amount of deductible. ***In essence, all you ever risk is the deductible, whether the vehicle has a high or low value.*** An example of this would be if you have an older vehicle with a $500 deductible on collision and the collision coverage costs $80 per year. You could reduce the collision deductible to $250, and the coverage would cost $110 per year. You are receiving $250 coverage for $30 per year which gives you a 8.3 year break-even period, which is greater than the ideal time frame for a break-even period. This is an example of a time to consider reducing your collision deductible. There are several schools of thought in relation to this subject. Let's look at some other possible ideas.

Another way to evaluate your coverage is as follows: Your vehicle is valued at $5,000 so you might consider raising the deductible to $1,000 to reduce the cost of the collision coverage while still having the major value of the vehicle covered. This will reduce your collision cost substantially. Another idea is to drop collision coverage altogether and save the collision coverage cost entirely but that isn't always a good idea. You have to again ask yourself the question, "Can I afford to replace my vehicle "out of pocket" today?" If the answer is yes and you are willing to take the risk, you may want to consider dropping collision coverage altogether.

When to Drop Collision Coverage

In my opinion, the only time that it is appropriate to drop collision coverage altogether, is not when the vehicle is paid off as some people think, but when the value of the vehicle, less the deductible, no longer makes it a wise investment. In other words, if the cost of coverage is too high in relation to the value of the vehicle and you would be able to replace the vehicle "out of pocket," then it's time to drop the collision coverage. For example, if your vehicle is worth $1,500 and you have a $250 deductible, you're only insuring a $1,250 value and the cost to insure is $150 per year. Is it worth it? Remember, you will always receive salvage value if the vehicle is a total loss. The salvage value would be around $200 to $300. The answer to this question may vary, based on your individual financial situation and the cost to insure versus the vehicle's value.

Classic and Antique Vehicles

Classic and antique vehicles are handled a little differently. These vehicles are insured on a stated value basis. The value is normally determined by an appraisal and insured for the amount of the appraisal. Most insurance companies will insure these vehicles; however, there are specialty insurers who can provide a far better rate on this type of coverage than most of the traditional casualty insurers. The way to find the best deal on this type of coverage is to look in classic car magazines for advertisements, or visit car shows and ask the car owners where they buy their insurance. After talking with several people, you will discover the best places to purchase this type of coverage.

5. Comprehensive Coverage

Very simply put, comprehensive coverage covers your vehicle for everything other than a collision, such as fire, theft, vandalism, wind, hail, etc. If you evaluate your risk as outlined in the previous section on collision coverage, you will make the right choice for comprehensive coverage as well. The same holds true in deciding on higher or lower deductibles. However, with comprehensive coverage, the cost structure is different in that comprehensive coverage usually isn't as expensive as collision coverage. You will need to shop the cost of different deductibles to discover what works best for you.

Normally a $100 to $250 deductible makes sense; however, it will also depend on the value of your vehicle and the rate structure for where you live. If you live in an area that experiences a high rate of auto theft, you will find that comprehensive coverage will be more expensive than in a low theft area.

In some areas you can purchase a glass waiver with your comprehensive coverage. Simply put, this is a rider attached to your policy that waives the comprehensive deductible if any glass is broken on the vehicle. This coverage not only covers windshields, but all windows, headlights and taillights as well. If you are interested in this option and it is available in your state, you would want to evaluate the cost of this optional glass coverage versus the amount of your deductible and how often you might have a glass loss. In some areas where glass breakage is a problem, it's a good idea to carry this coverage. You must remember, however, that your comprehensive coverage will cover a glass loss above the deductible. ***You are only buying back the deductible with the glass waiver.***

When considering dropping comprehensive coverage, you should use the same guidelines as outlined in the collision coverage section.

6. Miscellaneous Coverages

There are a number of coverages which people generally assume are included in their basic auto policy. These coverages include towing and road service, car rental reimbursement, accidental death, customization and non-factory equipment, travel trailers, campers, bedliners, etc.

In some policies towing and road service are automatically included, in others it is not. To evaluate this coverage you must consider several things. Do the benefits justify the cost? Some policies that include towing only allow $50 for towing coverage while others go up to $150 or higher. Something else to consider in evaluating your need for towing coverage is, "Do I maintain my vehicle, thereby reducing the chances of a breakdown and the need for towing coverage?" Remember, this also covers the cost of roadside services, e.g., being locked out of your vehicle, running out of gas, having a flat tire, etc. The guidelines for coverage may vary from state to state and company to company. Check the details related to this coverage prior to purchasing it to make sure you really need it.

Car rental reimbursement coverage covers you for a set dollar amount per day to pay the cost incurred to rent a vehicle if your vehicle is damaged due to a collision or comprehensive loss in excess of your deductible. There usually are several options to choose from, e.g., the number of days of coverage and the amount of coverage per day. Contrary to popular belief, this coverage doesn't cover you if your vehicle breaks down and is in the shop for repair. In addition, this coverage doesn't cover the cost of renting a vehicle for pleasure use.

If you rent a vehicle while on vacation or for pleasure use in the United States or Canada, most policies will extend your current auto coverage to the rental vehicle, therefore eliminating the need to buy the expensive coverage offered by the rental car companies. However, check with your present insurance company before making that assumption. This extension of coverage is different than the car rental reimbursement coverage discussed above. ***A note of caution;*** some car rental companies will charge you a fee plus a per diem charge if the vehicle is damaged and out of service for any length of time. They are charging you for loss of revenue for the time the vehicle is not being rented. Most auto policies ***will not*** pay these fees! Another way to cover this exposure is to rent the vehicle with a major credit card that covers material damage on rented vehicles. ***The latter option is the cleanest and most hassle free way to do it without buying the coverage offered by the car rental company.***

Please understand we are talking about two separate coverages. One is an automatic extension of your existing coverage to a rented vehicle, the other is coverage to pay the cost of renting a vehicle if you have a covered collision or comprehensive loss on your personal vehicle.

Something to consider before purchasing this coverage is, "If my vehicle is in the shop being repaired, do I have an extra vehicle in my household to use or can I get by with one less vehicle for a short period of time." If not, "Do I have friends or family members that I could depend on for the use of a spare vehicle?" The days of loaner cars have, for the most part, gone by the wayside.

Accidental death coverage, simply put, is life insurance on your auto policy. This coverage is only advisable to someone if they are unable to purchase life insurance separately. On the auto policy, accidental death coverage is limited to auto related death and is generally very expensive for the coverage received. In most cases, the money is better spent on regular life insurance.

Travel trailers and campers are not automatically covered on the auto policy, you must add them to the policy as riders. If you add this coverage to your policy, it carries the same deductibles as your collision and comprehensive coverages on your vehicle. The same guidelines should be used to evaluate the cost versus risk as previously outlined. Normally, the cost of this coverage is inexpensive.

Custom And Non-Factory Equipment

Customization and non-factory equipment coverage includes items such as bed liners for trucks, CB radios, KC lights, custom paint, van customization, etc. A good rule of thumb to determine if this coverage is needed is as follows. ***If it wasn't built by the factory or a factory replacement, it's not covered.*** Most companies offer coverage for these items at an affordable rate. Once again, risk versus cost versus the ability to pay out of pocket will help in making your decision.

As we close this chapter on coverages, it is my hope that you have gained the knowledge to define your needs and the ability to select the coverages that meet those needs without the help of an insurance agent. It is wise to learn how to make these choices on your own.

Chapter 2

The State Department of Insurance, A Major Resource

Chapter 2

The State Department of Insurance, A Major Resource

The state department of insurance is a major resource whose services are free. This is a vital resource that few insurance buyers take advantage of. Any questions you may have that are not covered in this book can be directed to the state department of insurance. In all 50 states, there is a state department of insurance that regulates the insurance industry in their particular state. The department not only oversees the operations of the insurance industry in the state, but helps to set guidelines, enforce laws, monitor complaints, and see that the insurance companies comply with their filings. Most important, they give protection to the insurance consumer. In addition, the department can supply valuable information to the consumer. This information includes, but is not limited to, the following: compile and supply rate comparisons (available in most states); complaint ratio list of companies doing business in the state; and general information about an insurance company. Functions of the department include managing the guarantee fund, taking action against insurance companies in violation of their filings or state law, rate and rule approval, licensing of agents and brokers, and many other related activities. ***Let's look at these items in more detail to see how they benefit you.***

Rate Comparisons

Most state insurance departments compile rate comparisons of all companies operating in the state. They will usually supply a comparison using several different scenarios to give you, the consumer, an idea as to how competitive a company is with other companies in the state. We will discuss how to use the rate comparisons in more detail in Chapter 3 which deals with selecting an insurance company.

Complaint Ratio List

The state department of insurance compiles what is called a ***"complaint ratio list."*** They compile information on all the insurance companies doing business in the state and rank them by their complaint ratio. This is how it works. Each company supplies the state department of insurance with the total number of policies they have in force. The department lists the company's name, total policies in force, the number of complaints lodged against the company and what the ratio of complaints is per 1,000 policies in force.

You must realize that not all complaints have merit, but it gives you a good indication of how responsive a company is to its policy holders, whether in policy service or claims adjusting. The companies you want to avoid are those with a ratio above .80 complaints per 1,000 policies in force. Look for companies with ratios under .45 complaints per 1,000 policies in force. ***Remember, a lower ratio means fewer complaints were filed.***

If a company you are interested in does not appear on the list, there are good reasons for it. One possible reason may be the state department of insurance omitted them in error, this sometimes happens. Another reason a company may not appear on the list is due to a high number of complaints lodged against them and they don't want the insurance buying public to know. If the insurance company fails to supply the department of insurance with the number of policies they have in force, it is impossible for the department to compile a complaint ratio list. Another reason a company may not appear on the list is because the company is a new entry in the state and has no track record to report. A call to the state department of insurance will answer these questions.

The State Guarantee Fund

The state department of insurance manages what is called the guarantee fund. This is a fund controlled by the state to which all insurance companies contribute.

If an insurance company becomes insolvent, money is available to pay outstanding claims and reimburse policy holders for any unearned premiums paid to the insolvent insurance company. The percentage of premiums paid by each insurance company is a relatively small percent of all premiums collected by the insurance company.

The bottom line is if you select an insurance company that becomes insolvent, you will eventually get your money back. However, it takes time, perhaps months, to get things resolved. In addition, the service you would receive from that company usually is very poor prior to their becoming insolvent. It is in your best interest to avoid any company that is having financial problems. In order to avoid a company in financial difficulty, you should check the A.M. Best rating for that particular company. There are several other similar insurance rating services and I'll provide a list with their phone numbers later. You can also research this information in your local library or check with your state department of insurance.

How and When to File a Complaint

It is always best to make an attempt at resolving a problem with your insurance company prior to filing a complaint. In any case, it's important to keep notes; e.g., dates, times and names of those you spoke with when trying to resolve a problem. ***If the insurance company is unable or unwilling to resolve the problem, then by all means, file a complaint with the state department of insurance.***

When filing a complaint, you must do it in writing, clearly outlining the problem. It is a good idea to list names, dates, times and whom you spoke with at the insurance company, and what their responses were. This will give your complaint more credibility than a poorly written or poorly documented complaint. Proper documentation will help to resolve the problem faster.

You should send your written complaint, certified mail, return receipt, to the state department of insurance in your state. You should expect a response within 30 days. Follow up with a phone call to the department if no response is received in that time frame. Also send a copy of your complaint to your insurance company and agent, if you have one.

I would like to say at this point the results you receive from the state department of insurance will depend on the state in which you live and the insurance company you insure with. The reason is simply this. In some states, the state department of insurance tends to look out for the interests of the industry; therefore, the consumer is not treated fairly. In most states, they are doing their job correctly, protecting the public from any misconduct of the insurance industry, as well as protecting the insurance industry from consumer misconduct. The individual company may or may not be on good terms with the state department of insurance; therefore, the complaint may be handled differently based on the company you insure with. Ideally, all complaints should be handled fairly for all parties involved!

Expected Results

The problem should be resolved within 30 to 60 days depending on the complexity of the complaint. You should also expect the complaint to be resolved within the laws that govern the affairs of the insurance industry in your state, as well as within the rules filed by your insurance company with the state.

Hopefully, you will never have to deal with this situation, but if you ever do, you now have the knowledge to handle it.

The following list contains the phone numbers for the state departments of insurance for all 50 states.

Alabama 334-269-3550
Alaska 907-269-7900
Arizona 602-912-8444
Arkansas 800-852-5494
California 800-927-4357
Colorado 303-894-7499
Connecticut 203-297-3867
Delaware 800-282-8611
Florida 904-022-3132
Georgia 404-656-2070
Hawaii 808-587-1234
Idaho 800-721-3272
Illinois 217-782-4515
Indiana 800-622-4461
Iowa 515-281-5705
Kansas 800-432-2484
Kentucky 502-564-3630
Louisiana 800-259-5300
Maine 207-624-8475
Maryland 800-492-6116
Massachusetts 617-521-7777
Michigan 517-373-9273
Minnesota 800-657-3602
Mississippi 800-562-2957
Missouri 800-726-7390
Montana 800-332-6148
Nebraska 402-471-2201
Nevada 800 992-0900
New Hampshire 800-852-341
New Jersey 800-446-7467
New Mexico 800-947-4722
New York 800-342-3736
North Carolina 800-662-7777
North Dakota 800-247-0560
Ohio 800-686-1526
Oregon 503-378-4484
Pennsylvania 717-787-2317
Rhode Island 401-277-2223
South Carolina 800-768-3467
South Dakota 605-773-3563
Tennessee 800-342-4029
Texas 800-252-3439
Utah 800-439-3805
Vermont 802-828-3301
Virginia 800-552-7945
Washington 800-562-6900
Washington D.C. 202-727-8000
West Virginia 800-642-9004
Wisconsin 800-236-8517
Wyoming 800-438-5768

Chapter 3

Selecting an Insurance Company

Chapter 3

Selecting an Insurance Company

Company Reputation

Many people will select an insurance company based solely on hearsay, or the fact that ***"back home they were a great company."*** As we will see, that is only a starting point for the following reasons.

An individual may have had a good experience in the past with an insurance company or an outstanding agent, therefore, they are satisfied with that company and the service received. That may not be a true reflection of the company in general. That way of thinking may be a big mistake, since the way things are handled where you live now may be different than "back home." Local reputation versus national reputation could be as different as night and day. I guarantee that you can find someone who has had a bad experience with the same insurance company and after talking with them you wouldn't consider doing business with that company. ***Personal opinion or past experiences have little to do with selecting the right insurance company.***

You need to use the information outlined in Chapter 2 as part of the selection process, as well as the information outlined in this chapter. The primary reason for the selection process is insurance companies divide their operating territory and have different people in charge of various regions or territories. The attitude of each region can be quite different, even within the same company. This attitude and style of management will be reflected all the way down the line and affect the way claims are handled and policies serviced, as well as the agents' attitudes. In addition, you have state regulations to deal with in each region that may influence the way situations are handled. However, such regulations should affect all insurance companies doing business in that region in the same way.

Price, Service and Size

While price isn't the only factor to consider, it is a major one. Most important factors about an insurance company are reflected in the price of their product!

If you are considering an insurance company that has been doing business in your state for at least five years, you should have enough history to make several conclusions on price alone.

The first conclusion is based on customer selection and payment of claims. You must ask yourself, "Is the insurance company being careful in customer selection and being fair on claims settlements?" If they have a competitive rate structure, chances are they are careful in customer selection and claims adjusting. ***You don't want an insurance company that overpays claims or isn't customer selective; those errors will be reflected in the rate structure.***

A reason for the five year time frame is many insurance companies new in an area will, for the first few years, sell their coverages at artificially low rates to attract new customers. This type of activity will usually be corrected within the five years. Here's how it works. A company comes into an area with low rates. After a few years, their rates become as artificially high as they were low. A series of large rate increases are made in an attempt to regain the premium lost initially in the early years. The reason for this is that they lost too much money in their entry into the state and are now cutting their losses short. This activity causes them to lose preferred customers and then be left with an undesirable customer base so their problems escalate. In some cases, they will withdraw from the state altogether and discontinue writing new business or servicing existing customers. Increased problems are due to customers with good loss history leaving for other companies with less expensive rates. The company is left with a majority of customers who have a poor loss history and cannot obtain coverage at a lower rate. This is called ***"adverse selection."*** The insurance company finally withdraws from the state entirely to end their unprofitable venture leaving many customers to obtain coverage from other companies.

The other possibility is if after five years an insurance company continues to offer low rates, chances are they're doing things right and worth investigating further. This is the type of company that will continue to offer low rates for many years to come and that's the type of insurance company you want. ***Just a word of caution;*** If the insurance company you currently have is competitive one year and not the next and then competitive the next year, etc., chances are the management of the company lacks direction and the necessary skills required to successfully manage the company. If you experience this kind of rate fluctuation, it's time to look for a consistently managed company. I have seen both types of companies in my many years of experience and found that companies improperly managed tend to remain small and provide poor service along with non-competitive rates.

Service

Initially you should check the company out as outlined in Chapter 2. You can also talk to several people who have this particular company and get feedback on their experiences, although this is not always a reliable source as mentioned earlier. If you wish to continue your investigation, you could visit the claims office that would service your account and ask to speak with the claims manager. If you have a good feel for people, you will see the company's attitude reflected in the claims manager's attitude; an attitude that will be reflected throughout the claims process.

In my opinion, probably the best way to check out a company's claims procedures is to visit several auto body repair shops in your community. Ask the shop managers about the company you are considering. They will be able to tell you how hard or easy your prospective company is to work with. These visits will tell you a great deal about how the insurance company pays claims and give you an overall indication of how they deal with their customers, as well as others who may be involved in your claim.

Bigger Isn't Always Better

In the past you were usually correct in your assumption that the bigger the insurance company, the better; but not anymore! The giant companies of today are becoming the dinosaurs of tomorrow simply because they are unable and, in some cases unwilling, to change fast enough to provide the kind of business environment needed for the future. The newer, smaller and smarter companies are meeting that challenge. They are appearing on the scene and providing better rates and ease of service to their customers. More on this subject in Chapter 5.

Size isn't an issue of importance if other things such as price, claims settlement, financial strength, and the customer's ability to communicate with the company are in order.

Twelve Questions Insurance Buyers Never Ask, But Should

1. What Is Your Company's Expense Ratio?

Most people, including agents, don't even know what an expense ratio is or how it affects them, so allow me to explain. The expense ratio is the percentage of every premium dollar paid that is used to cover the expenses of operating the company. It's obvious that the higher the ratio, the higher the cost of insurance.

Some of the older, big name companies have expense ratios as high as 26%, while some newer, smaller and smarter companies have ratios in the single digits! ***Your obvious question is, " How do some companies accomplish the lower ratios?"*** The answer lies in the fact that many companies have cut their overhead to the bone through technology, reduction of personnel and, of course, the elimination of the agency force. This will be covered in more detail in Chapter 5. ***With the knowledge you receive in this book, you can purchase insurance without the aid of an agent and the difference in expense ratio will be converted to <u>cash in your pocket!</u>***

2. What Is Your Company's Current A.M. Best Rating and Their Ratings Over the Past Three Years?

An area of utmost importance when selecting an insurance company is their A.M. Best rating. There are several other agencies that rate insurance companies besides A.M. Best and after a brief explanation of their value, I will give their names and telephone numbers. These rating agencies rate insurance companies on a number of different areas. These include, but are not limited to, the company's financial strength, quality and effectiveness of management, results of marketing efforts and penetration in their area of operation, quality and effectiveness of their agency or direct marketing operations, and their overall ability to manage a sound insurance company.

Any company with an A.M. Best rating lower than an ***"A"*** should be avoided no matter what the agent or company representative tells you. There are reasons the company was downgraded from an ***"A" or "A++"*** rating. These reasons could be many; ranging from an insurance company's inability to add to their reserves (money set aside to pay claims), the inability to grow reserves to a safe level, the inability to grow policies in force, or management errors.

The point I'm trying to make is if an insurance company has been rated below the ***"A"*** rating in the past three years, there is a good reason for it. If the insurance company regains the ***"A"*** rating after losing it and retains it for at least three years, chances are the problems have been corrected and it is a safe company to purchase insurance from. The only exception to this rule is in the case of an insurance company that has been in trouble, and has had a ***"cash infusion"*** from another company. What I mean by a ***"cash infusion"*** is that another company has come to the rescue of the company in trouble. They will supply the needed cash to restore the financial health of the company, and make the necessary management changes to correct the problems that created the downgrade initially. This is a good indication that the company underwent some major marketing and management restructuring in order to secure the cash needed to operate. In such a case, you would be safe with the company in spite of their past.

Rating Companies Include The Following

A.M. Best Company 908-439-2200
Demotech, Inc. 614-761-8602
Duff & Phelps, Inc. 312-368-3157
Fitch Investors Service 212-908-0500
Moody's Investors Services 212-553-0377

Standard & Poors 212-208-1527
Weiss Research, Inc. 800-289-9222

NOTE: There may be a fee involved when requesting a company rating.

I realize these rating companies rate life and health insurance, as well as casualty insurance companies, but I want to supply you with as many resources as possible on this subject.

3. What Is Your Company's Complaint Ratio?

In Chapter 2 we discussed how the complaint ratio works, so I won't spend a great deal of time on it now, other than to say it is a vital sign of an insurance company's ability to provide the service you are paying for. ***Remember, you want an insurance company to have a complaint ratio of .45 or less complaints per 1,000 policies in force, and avoid companies with a ratio over .80.***

4. How Many Auto and Homeowner's Policies Does Your Insurance Company Have in My State?

In general, the larger the presence of an insurance company in the state, the greater the chance of rate stability. The reason for this is with a larger policy base they are better equipped to handle a catastrophic loss or a series of such losses in an efficient manner. The other major advantage is with a greater presence they are more likely to have adequate claims and customer support to handle any losses you may have, or any other needs that may arise. The exception to this would be a company with national reputation that has recently moved into your state; the assumption being that they will be growing as their marketing efforts bring results. Policies in force would not be an issue then.

Another consideration is if a company having been in the state five years or longer, continues to have a small policy base, low complaint ratio and a competitive premium structure, it could be a company that will meet your needs.

5. How Long Has Your Insurance Company Been Doing Business in My State?

If the insurance company has been doing business for five years or more in your state and all the other criteria are to your satisfaction, chances are it is a safe company to insure with. If the company has been in business for five years or more but is new to your state, you should be aware of the following.

Many insurance companies will enter a market with artificially low rates to attract new business, as discussed earlier. Upon entering the market, they know they will lose X number of dollars and consider it as part of the cost of doing business. Later, if not managed properly, they will become as artificially high in their rate structure as they were low. An indication of possible large rate adjustments would be to look at their expense ratio as discussed earlier. If their ratio is low, 15% or less, it is likely that their rate structure will remain attractive. However, if the ratio is above the 15% to 20% range, chances are they are cash flow underwriting and rates will go up. Cash flow underwriting is a term used for insurance companies that come into an area with artificially low rates to attract customers with the intention of raising rates later.

6. Who Adjusts the Claims?

This is a very important question. Some insurance companies have their own claims adjusting personnel while others use contract adjustors. There are advantages and disadvantages to both.

Company adjustors have a tendency to look out for the best interest of their employer, the insurance company. Often, they will not be as liberal on adjusting a claim knowing they are employees of the insurance company. On the other hand, they know that if you, the customer, is not satisfied with the outcome, the insurance company may lose a good customer. Therefore the adjuster, may be more inclined to go the extra mile to assure customer satisfaction. I've seen both scenarios carried to the extreme.

Contract adjustors are not as concerned with the amount of payment made or with customer satisfaction. They work for several insurance companies and in general, are not as concerned for you as a company adjustor might be. However, many contract adjustors tend to be more liberal in adjusting the claim because they lack company loyalty. So, while they may not use the best public relations skills, they may allow more money to settle the claim. There are pros and cons on either side. Provisions in the policy protect you as to what is covered and how the claim is to be adjusted. The end result being that you will eventually receive a fair settlement, no matter who adjusts the claim.

The above information is written with regard to dealing with your own insurance company. If you file a claim against someone else's insurance company, you have no choice in the type of adjustor you will be dealing with. Filing a claim against another person's insurance company will be discussed in Chapter 4.

7. What Other Lines of Insurance Does Your Company Sell in My Community?

Does the insurance company sell homeowner's insurance or excess liability policies, life insurance or any other line of insurance you may be interested in? This is important since many companies offer multi-policy discounts. For example, some companies offer a discount on your auto insurance if you have your homeowner's or a similar policy with them. These discounts can be as little as 5% or as much as 15% to 20%. If they offer more than one line of insurance, it's quite probable that they are committed to your area. If they were to experience negative results for a period of time, as companies often do, they are less likely to withdraw from your community.

8. When Did Your Company Have Their Last Rate Increase and What Was the Percentage of Increase?

If one or more of the major insurance companies have had a recent rate increase, you can count on most companies following suit within six to eight months. The percentage of that increase will vary, but it will happen.

An example of this would be if your current carrier recently had a 10% increase in rates and the new company you are considering hasn't had an increase for a year or more. With all coverages and usage factors rated equally, if the new company's rate is 20% lower than what you are offered for renewal with your current company, you should assume that the company you are considering will also have a 10% increase before your next renewal. ***You still have a 10% savings for the long term!***

Some insurance companies are consistently lower in cost over the long term. This is the type of insurance company you want to find. Also when you shop, remember, if your policy is not properly rated, e.g., comparable coverages, distance to and from work, business or pleasure use, age of drivers, etc., your comparison will not be accurate. ***You have to compare all rating factors equally between companies.***

9. What Happens to My Rates If I Have an Accident That Is My Fault?

This is a very important question to ask. The cost will vary greatly from company to company! Over the years, I've encountered companies that charge a small percentage for a three year period, say 10% for the vehicle involved in the accident, companies that forgive the first accident and don't increase the rates at all, and I've also encountered companies that will charge a 50% surcharge of the premium on all vehicles in the household! A more acceptable penalty would be a 20% to 30% surcharge for the vehicle involved in the accident for no more than three years. ***As I said, these penalties can vary greatly!***

The other part of this question is, "What is the dollar limit that triggers the surcharge?"

For example, you are involved in a minor accident and the damage to both vehicles was in the $1,000 range. At today's prices, $1,000 may not even be visible damage. The question is, "At what dollar amount of damage will the surcharge be applied to my policy?" This can vary from as little as a few hundred dollars to forgiveness of the first accident altogether! **I can't overemphasize the importance of this question.**

10. What Happens If I Receive One or More Traffic Citations?

This is also very important! Some insurance companies will check your driving record every 6 to 12 months looking for traffic citations. Others will check only if you have an accident or are adding another vehicle to your policy.

The potential for a surcharge based on citations varies widely between companies to the extent that one or more citations will not have an effect on your rates, or you could have surcharges for each citation. With some companies, these surcharges can add up to 50%+ of additional premium, depending on the number and type of citations! If you have a major citation such as driving while intoxicated or leaving the scene of an accident, etc., most insurance companies will cancel your policy or place you in a standard company at substantially higher rates!

Obviously, the best way to avoid these problems is to drive carefully and avoid citations. However, if you do receive one, check to see if your state offers a driving class you can attend which will remove the citation from your driving record. This class may take a Saturday away from you, but it could save you big dollars on your auto insurance premiums in the future. You must realize if you are involved in an accident that is your fault and you attend the driving class, the citation will be removed but the insurance company will still have to pay for the accident. Therefore, your rates will still be affected. ***Attending the class doesn't take your insurance company off the hook!***

Citation surcharges are one of the hidden and potentially high cost factors when buying auto insurance that most people do not investigate! These surcharges can vary widely from company to company and should not be overlooked in the shopping process.

I can't overemphasize the value of a clean driving record! Equally important is having a clean claims history. Insurance companies look at items such as towing and glass claims, or even losses that weren't your fault, as part of the overall customer selection process. A clean claims history can make the difference between getting preferred rates as opposed to standard rates.

11. Does Your Company Have a Commissioned Sales Force and If So, Are They With or Without Sales Quotas?

Your initial reaction to this question more than likely is, "Who cares!" Well, no one does but it can have an effect not only on the rates you pay but also on the service you receive. There are several ways in which to evaluate this matter.

If you purchase your insurance from a company that doesn't have a commissioned sales force or agents and you deal directly with an employee of the company, not only do you remove a layer of people to deal with but also ***a level of expense, reducing the cost of your policy.*** The idea that an agent is looking out for your best interest is no longer true to the degree it once was. The agent of today has very little authority to exercise his or her own judgment on your behalf. Unfortunately, they have become mere puppets of the insurance company to the extent that they can mirror only the desires of the insurance company. This is not true 100% of the time, but is most of the time. It's not that the agent doesn't want to get things done for you; he or she just can't. ***The days of the agent being "your agent" are long past!*** Now they are agents of the insurance company, looking out for their company's best interest first and unfortunately, yours last! The agent cannot do anything for you that the company wouldn't do for you without the agent.

How much time do you spend each year on the phone with your agent? You will discover that if you are an average insurance customer you probably spend less than one hour per year talking to your agent. If you didn't have an agent, you would still spend that same amount of time talking to a company representative on the phone or by direct communication on the computer. ***So my question to you, the insurance buyer is, "Why have an agent?" The premium savings obtained by not having an agent are substantial, and the knowledge required to do it yourself is fairly simple.***

Many agents make six figure incomes and work less than 40 hours per week! Who do you think supports the golf courses? Quite frankly, it's the best part-time job a person could have! However, in all fairness to the agents, you must realize in the first five to eight years of his or her career, the agent worked 60 to 80 hours per week to build the agency and was doing it for less money. There is a huge price to pay in building a successful insurance agency!

Sales Quotas, Who Cares? You Should for the Following Reasons

A company that sets sales quotas for its agency force, whether these quotas are specific or implied should be avoided. The reason for this statement is these companies will allow business to be written for the sake of meeting quotas. Agents will fudge on the rules or ask for exceptions that should not be granted but are. This adds business to the books at rates so low that the insurance companies will never make a profit. Thus, it contributes to adverse selection. Adverse selection is when an insurance company has business on the books they can't remove or make profitable. You and I are paying for those money losing policies that should never have been written in the first place. ***In most cases, adverse selection is the result of mismanagement.*** The quality customers will leave to go to other insurance companies who have lower rates, and the money losing customers will not be able to change companies because of their loss history. The result is the insurance company ends up with a bad book of business that cannot be easily changed. I'm not saying it's impossible, but close to it.

This type of behavior will vary from company to company, but you can avoid it altogether by not selecting an insurance company with a commissioned sales force. Another thing you should be aware of is that most, if not all insurance companies, discriminate in customer selection. Sounds shocking but true! The industry won't admit it, but I'll explain how it's done.

Assume that your underwriting situation doesn't fit the narrow guidelines that the insurance company dictates. You may have had a driver in the household who received a citation or had an accident that is chargeable and is within the time frame of the insurance company's concern. Therefore, you are not eligible for the best rate available. This would pose a problem if you were adding a vehicle to your policy with the same company, or going to another insurance company altogether. The underwriting department will give exceptions at will to whoever they want, and withhold them from whomever they wish. You might ask, "What are the guidelines for this behavior, it doesn't make sense?" You're right, it doesn't.

There are several things that the company looks at in evaluating your account. One is, "Do you have supporting business with the company or do you just have your auto insurance with them?" Giving the insurance company all of your insurance business is what they really want, especially your life insurance! You could be in an identical situation and carry life insurance with the company and they would grant that exception as opposed to not carrying life insurance with them and having your request denied! ***I've seen this happen many times! In my opinion, it's close to blackmail.***

Another thing that will make a difference as to whether you get an exception or not is your agent. If your agent has a good reputation with the insurance company, or is a big life insurance producer and making money for the insurance company, your request for an exception will have a better chance of being granted.

Another area is the personal judgment of the underwriter. One underwriter may allow something that another underwriter would not allow given the same set of circumstances. It's all a matter of personal preference with the underwriter.

As I've pointed out, it is all arbitrary and depends on a number of things, some of which having nothing to do with you! That is how the industry avoids being pinned down and held accountable on any given case. ***Stop and think; you're still you!*** No matter what agent you have, which underwriter reviews your account, or whether you have additional business with the company, you and your situation remain the same! ***Yet, the way the account is handled is discriminatory to the insurance buyer based on personalities, favoritism toward an agent, and politics in general!***

The best way to avoid this type of behavior is to deal only with an insurance company that does not have an agency force! The less people involved, the fairer the treatment. This will enable you to buy your auto insurance at a lower price since you have removed an excess level of expense and eliminated a level of hassle.

12. How Many Levels of Quota / Commission Management are There?

If you deal with an agent and the agency force has commissioned district or regional management, the cost and bureaucracy increases.

An example would be as follows: you have an agency force that has to sell a certain number of policies or has a production quota. Then they have a manager that has quotas and he has a manager who also has quotas. You now have three levels of either commission and/or production requirements that only add to the cost of your auto insurance, and you receive nothing for it!

Many agents and district or regional managers who are commissioned sales people make six figure incomes after expenses. It's not that they didn't work hard to get where they are, they did. ***What I am saying is times are changing and you, the insurance consumer, can learn a little and save a lot by becoming your own agent.*** Change is coming whether we want it or not, so you may as well learn now and do what is needed in order to prepare for the future!

The insurance industry is working hard at changing to meet the challenges that lay ahead, but it is like trying to turn a battleship around in a bathtub. These companies have contracts with agents and managers that they cannot easily terminate without legal considerations. Another set of problems facing the major carriers is the fact that they are not prepared to handle their business without the agency force. ***I believe, contrary to what the industry says, if they could manage without the agent, the majority of agents would be gone tomorrow!***

One major insurance company recently offered new contracts to its agency force that would cut their commissions by approximately 33%. It is not yet mandatory that they sign the new contract, but it may happen soon. This same company reorganized its district management by reducing the number of district managers and giving the remaining district managers more agents to look after. Most of the major insurance companies are frantically trying to reorganize and automate in order to reduce their expense ratios so they can compete. ***This is good for the insurance consumer in the long run. To sum it up, working without an agent, in itself, should reduce your cost by as much as 15% or more.***

Selecting an Agent

Five Qualities Your Agent Should Possess to do the Kind of Job You Deserve

If you're still not comfortable purchasing auto insurance without an agent, let me explain how to select a qualified agent.

1. Does the agent have at least five years experience?

The last person you want as an insurance agent is a new agent. Not that he or she wouldn't make a good agent, it's just that because of the way the industry is changing you want one with experience. You not only want an agent with experience in the insurance industry, but preferably with the company you have selected. The five year time frame gives the agent valuable experience and also shows stability on the part of the agent which is very important. In addition, it adds to the agent's credibility with the insurance company. If a problem was to arise, an experienced agent may be able to do things for you that a new agent could not do. If any agent could make a difference, it would be the experienced agent. However, as with many insurance companies, the agent has virtually no say as to what the company does. In most cases, the insurance company will move faster for you than for the agent. Usually a complaint made by the consumer directly to the company will receive greater attention than an agent trying to solve the same problem. Many times I've told a customer that I've done all that I can, why not call the company personally. Guess what? They were able to get the problem resolved with one phone call that I couldn't resolve with many calls. ***The consumer's voice has clout!***

2. Is the Agent an Award Winning or Superstar Agent?

If you walk into a prospective agent's office and see numerous plaques on the wall, chances are you may want to select another agent. The main reason for this is most property and casualty companies push their life insurance products on the auto insurance buyer, via the auto insurance agent. Most, if not all awards, are for life insurance production. I can't remember the last time there was an auto insurance production contest. What's wrong with awards for life insurance production you may ask? Let me take this opportunity to explain what I believe is wrong with them.

Most major insurance companies keep their agency force for the purpose of selling life insurance to their auto insurance customers. Usually their products are far more expensive than life only companies. If you want to purchase life insurance, you are far better off going to someone who is a life insurance broker and can shop rates for you. There are several brokers that use 800 numbers, and with a single phone call, can supply you with five or more quotes from top rated companies at greatly reduced prices. They can do this because they have cut out the middleman, the agent. Major casualty and life companies with agents pay commissions as high as 100% or more of the first year's premium plus smaller percentages for renewals beyond that time frame. It's expensive for an agent to come to your home to sell you a policy; and you're paying a much higher premium for that service!

I believe in life insurance but you need to do some careful shopping before you buy. Usually term insurance is the best for the money. More information on this subject in the life insurance supplement, ***"The Great Life Insurance Hoax,"*** which is offered at the back of this book.

So back to my original point. If the agent is a top award winner, you can almost bet at some point you will be pressured to buy life insurance. Unfortunately, many people buy these inferior life insurance products that are not always suited to meet their needs from this type of agent. It makes a person of conscience ill knowing what is taking place. Many people who have bought these policies from prior agents have said to me, ***"I don't know why I bought the policy."*** I too, have wondered the same!

3. Does the Agent Have an Office With Low Visibility?

You don't want an agent who has an office on a neighborhood corner or in a shopping center. Generally, a high percentage of ***"walk in"*** business is the least desirable type of client an agent can have. If an agent has high exposure to ***"walk in"*** business, he or she will be occupied with customers that require a great deal of time and attention, and the agent will experience a high turnover in his or her customer base. This type of clientele will cause the agent to do a greater amount of non-productive work, reducing time which could be better spent doing things of value, such as reviewing your account periodically to ensure your policies are rated correctly, that you're receiving all the discounts you are entitled to, and as things change in the company, you benefit from those changes.

An agent located in an office complex that is harder to locate is the preferred location. The major advantage to this location is ***"walk in"*** business is almost non-existent; therefore, the agent has more time to service your account because the problems listed above are eliminated. The other advantage is the agent who is hard to find by the casual shopper has to be a good agent in order to build his or her agency and survive. They have to build their agency by working hard and giving excellent service! In many instances, the agent on the street corner lacks the incentive to go out and find new customers. They would rather wait for the customers to come to them. ***This attitude will be reflected in the quality of service you receive.***

4. Does the Agent Have Proper Staffing?

You want to be sure the agent's office is properly staffed so that your account will be handled promptly and efficiently. Don't expect to be treated as though you are the only customer, but in most cases, your call should be returned the same business day or at least an attempt made by the agent or his or her staff to do so.

Some signs of an improperly staffed office are as follows: 1) you're put on hold for more than two minutes; 2) you get a recording or voice mail during business hours; or 3) you have delays in getting paperwork or claims processed in a timely manner. This is the type of office you want to avoid! The best way to detect proper staffing is to visit the office personally and observe the general atmosphere of the office. Does the environment seem hurried? Are calls waiting on hold? Do the desks look cluttered and unorganized, or is there a sense of calm and control? ***It should be obvious which type of office you would want to do business with!***

5. Does the Agent Have Time to Personally Meet You?

If the prospective agent doesn't have time to meet with you personally, chances are you may want to select another agent. While it's true that a staff member can properly service your account in the future, you should meet the agent initially so you get a feel for what type of person he or she is. ***Remember, the staff's attitude and office environment are a reflection of the agent.***

Additional Information On Agent Selection

What About Recommendations from Friends?

A recommendation from a friend is a good starting place. If your friend is happy with the agent, chances are you will be too. However, you would be wise to use due diligence as outlined in this section, and not go solely on the friend's recommendation.

Phone or Mail Solicitation

This is probably the worst way to buy auto or any other type of insurance.

Generally, you will find new agents doing this type of solicitation to get started in the business. There is nothing wrong with it, but you won't get the quality and experience you want. Let's face it, that's how I started, but that was over 20 years ago! You would be better served using other methods to shop for your auto insurance, e.g., the Internet, the use of 800 numbers, and other methods of discount mass marketing which are replacing the traditional methods of today.

Many times through error, inexperience or outright fraud, the agent will quote you an incorrect rate. When the policy is issued, you find the rate quoted versus the rate of the issued policy is different! Has this ever happened to you? Often it turns out you would have been better off to have stayed with your prior insurance company than make the change. Some agents do this on purpose knowing that most people, because of pride, will pay the higher price of the new company rather than return to their prior insurance company. This kind of activity is common practice, especially among new agents.

As I've said before, the days of the auto insurance agent are numbered, so you might as well be prepared to do it yourself.

What about Independent Agents Versus Captive Agents?

The difference between the two types of agents is the captive agent works on an exclusive contract with one company while the independent agent usually represents several companies. Some advantages to using independent agents include their ability to shop the market for the best possible rates and coverages for your situation. They are not bound to any one company, therefore their loyalty is to you, not the insurance company. A captive agent's loyalty is to the insurance company. The major reason for not providing what you need is the limited scope of products and choices he or she has to offer. The major disadvantage of an independent agent is some agents will switch you from company to company, telling you they found a cheaper rate, when in reality they are looking out for their commission checks. Let me explain what I mean. Normally, when a policy is written, the agent receives a commission. When the policy renews, the agent again receives a commission. The problem is the renewal commission is smaller than the new business commission, so by switching you from company to company the agent earns a higher commission.

Commissions can be as high as 20% for new business dropping to only 10% for renewals. ***Stop and think, the agent can double the commission by switching you from company to company!*** If your independent agent changes your auto insurance company often, chances are that's what's happening!

No Agent Is the Ideal

I cannot emphasize this enough! The agency force of the future will not provide the kind of service you are accustomed to today. Why then should you have an agent? If you can do investing without a full commissioned broker, do your banking without the assistance of a live teller, then why do you need the services of an agent for your auto insurance? As stated earlier, the main purpose of this book is to prepare you for, and supply you with, the tools and knowledge necessary to do it yourself.

Loyalty, Is There Any?

Most people assume that if they stay with an insurance company for a long time, they will create a loyalty between the insurance company and themselves. That is true to a minor degree. Many companies do offer programs such as longevity discounts up to 15%+, for customers insured with the company for X number of years. However, a majority of the time you're not getting a good rate in those first X number of years. It's like a jewelry sale where they cut the price in half on an already overpriced product and after the discount it's still overpriced. The only other possible advantage for longevity with an insurance company is in the event you need an underwriting exception for a situation that has occurred. An example of an exception would be as follows. You purchase an additional vehicle, and when you request the vehicle be added to your policy, you discover that the speeding citation you received last year will keep you from getting the best possible rate. Your agent could request an exception from the company and, if granted, the company overlooks the citation and gives you the lower rate. This would be expected if you have been with an insurance company for a long time and your account has been profitable. However, I've seen cases of longtime clients not getting this kind of service because the company decided no more exceptions, leaving the customer out in the cold!

Each company files its rules with the state department of insurance. Anything they do differently from what is filed is an exception. They don't like to give exceptions but if enough pressure is applied they will. One reason they don't like to give exceptions is they are audited by the insurance department and have to give an accounting for all exceptions given. In spite of this fact, they do give exceptions to whomever they wish, whenever they wish.

What you and I consider loyalty to be in a relationship is almost non-existent in the insurance business. The name of the game now is big business, big dollars and bottom line results! It has to be that way because the business of getting your insurance dollars has become so competitive and changes so rapidly that the days of loyalty and relationships are a thing of the past. ***I would say for the most part, loyalty to you from the insurance company means little to nothing, and should not be considered as a factor in changing companies***

Agent loyalty is quite a different matter. The agent is paid on a commission only basis, and therefore, is more concerned about your welfare. If you are loyal to a good agent, that agent will be loyal to you doing all he or she can to service your account. Agents possessing a loyal attitude probably represent 60% to 70% of all agents in the business.

Remember, the agent is a puppet of the insurance company and there is very little he or she can do for you that the insurance company wouldn't allow you to do without an agent. Also, remember the role of the agent today will become far different in the future. ***So again, it's time to look out for yourself and consider acting as your own agent!***

How to Resolve a Problem with Your Insurance Company

In addition to the information in Chapter 2, here are a few more helpful hints. When trying to resolve a claims related problem with the insurance company, you should go directly to a claims supervisor if your agent or claims adjuster was unable to resolve the problem. You are entitled to an accounting of what was offered to you versus the actual damage incurred. Documentation is key for your case. Many times your efforts will pay off if you are willing to take the time to do a little leg work.

Unfortunately, your agent doesn't have the time or authority needed to do the additional work required to resolve a disputed claim. We will go into more detail on the claims issue in Chapter 4.

To resolve a dispute with the insurance company in a non-claim related matter, you must first plead your case with your agent or company representative. ***Your agent or representative is, by no means, the final authority!*** If you don't think you are getting the results you desire, ask to speak to a district manager or supervisor. You have to understand the layers of management above an agent or representative. For the most part, management is not skilled in dealing with the public and unable to stand up to the public. It's easy for this level of management to tell an agent or representative "no," but to tell an unhappy customer "no" is quite a different story! Many times I've gone to bat for a customer, only to be told by my superior "no!" Then the customer, unhappy with my results, calls and talks to the same person that turned me down, and gets what they want! ***As I mentioned before, a customer can get more done than an agent can, so why pay an agent to do something you can do better!*** The truth is the district and regional managers don't have the skills to handle a confrontation by an unhappy customer, and in many cases, they will back down. This is especially true with underwriters who make decisions with no regard as to how it will affect you personally. Their only concern is the bottom line, knowing the agent is the one who has to deal with the customer. So my advice is that you go beyond your agent, try to speak to an underwriter directly and plead your case, providing it's an underwriting problem. Chances are you will win all or part of what you want.

The least effective thing you can say is ***"I'll sue,"*** this is heard all the time. The most effective thing you can say is, ***"I'll file a complaint with the state department of insurance."*** They prefer you didn't for two reasons. First, your complaint, valid or not, will increase their complaint ratio; secondly, they don't want the scrutiny of the state department of insurance and therefore, are more willing to give you what you want and avoid the results of a complaint.

What Can an Insurance Company Find Out About You?

When you apply for coverage with an insurance company, your application is subject to an underwriting review. They look at all sorts of information, such as how far you drive to work one way, job stability, ages and driving records of all drivers in your household, loss history, etc. Did you know they also look at your credit report? One of the newest underwriting tools is doing a credit profile. Your profile is scored based on an unknown criteria, unknown not only to me, but to most individual underwriters involved in using this method. The underwriter never sees your credit report, they only see the score that your credit report generates. They don't even know how the score is calculated! ***Many times your score will determine if a policy is issued.*** The industry has proven over the years that people with a good credit history will generally be a better risk, regardless of driving records. This method has been used in Europe for years and has proven successful.

In addition, most applicants do not realize that all the information relating to claims filed with your prior insurance carriers is available to the new insurance company through various private reporting agencies. Most major insurance companies subscribe to these services for a fee. Insurance companies supply the reporting company with data about your claims history, then when you attempt to change companies, the new company can order a report to review your claims history. It works like a credit bureau, only rather than credit history being compiled, it's your claims history. It's not a bad system and helps keep people honest.

As in everything, mistakes are made. It is in your best interest to keep your own file on your claims history. The reason for this is just as credit bureaus make mistakes, so do these reporting agencies. An accurate claims history could be invaluable to you if you attempt to change insurance companies and are denied coverage due to incorrect information on your report. You can, occasionally, request an experience letter regarding your claims history by contacting the underwriting department of your current insurance company. An experience letter is an accounting of your loss history with your current insurance company. ***This is a good idea to do prior to changing insurance companies.*** If there is an error in your claims history, you can be on top of it and resolve it before it causes you a problem. Most states require the insurance company to respond to your request within a set number of days from receipt of your request.

Another underwriting tool used by insurance companies is conducting an investigation. This isn't done as often as it once was; however, in some cases at the company's discretion, they will conduct one. This investigation usually consists of verifying your employment, talking to you or your neighbors and doing a more in-depth search into your habits and lifestyle. This may also include verifying the use of the vehicle(s) you insure and the number of drivers in your household. It's really nothing to be concerned with if you have supplied the insurance company with accurate information; although, the issue of privacy may be raised at this point. ***How far should an insurance company be allowed to go in determining if you are an acceptable driving risk?***

You must realize not everything outlined in this chapter will be the same with all insurance companies. You must choose which issues are most important to you in selecting an insurance company. Some issues will be of lesser or greater importance and the method of prioritizing will be different for each individual.

Your knowing the information in this chapter will give you the upper hand in shopping for and obtaining the best possible deal on your auto insurance! Good luck in your search!

Chapter 4

How to Settle a Claim Fairly

Chapter 4

How to Settle a Claim Fairly

The information in this chapter is accurate to the best of my knowledge. The problem encountered in writing this chapter is dealing with the fact that claims adjusting varies from state to state. The resulting settlement will vary depending on the verbiage of your policy and the laws that govern insurance in the state where you reside. If you are uncomfortable with any of the advice given in this chapter, please do not act upon it until you have had the opportunity to do the proper research.

In the settlement process people often feel the insurance company is out to give them the short end of the stick. Unfortunately, sometimes that happens. I strongly believe that the claims process is important and that's why I have chosen to devote an entire chapter to it. In this chapter I'll explain to you some of the "ins" and "outs" of the claims process.

1. Settling a Bodily Injury Liability Claim

If you are involved in an accident and the other party is at fault, you are entitled to be made whole financially through the other party's insurance company. If the party at fault doesn't carry auto liability insurance and you carry ***uninsured*** motorist coverage, you would be compensated through your own insurance company. If the party at fault carried liability insurance, but their coverage limit wasn't enough, the excess amount would be covered by the ***underinsured*** motorist coverage on your policy, providing that you carry such coverage.

Bodily injury liability, uninsured and underinsured motorist coverages are designed to pay for the following:

1. Actual medical expenses
2. Actual wages lost as a result of the accident

3. Expenses for mileage to and from the doctor, therapy, trips to the store for items you require and any other miles driven as a result of the accident.

4. Compensation for any temporary or permanent disability. This could be as minor as a few days missed from work, to a major disability such as loss of a limb, loss of hearing, loss of mental capacity, or physical disablement.

5. Compensation for pain and suffering as a result of the accident.

This brings to mind the question, ***"How do I know the insurance company is being fair with me in these areas?"*** I hope by the time you finish this chapter you will have learned enough to adequately handle this type of claim on your own, without an attorney, and get top dollar in the process! Let's look at these areas one at a time.

1. Actual Medical Expenses

This is fairly simple. Keep records of your doctor, therapy, drug, hospital and any other related expenses incurred for medical treatment as a result of the accident.

Most medical practitioners will wait for payment until after you have settled your claim. This should be worked out in advance of services being rendered. If they won't wait for you to settle with the insurance company, then you may want to look for another health provider. The reason for this is when you settle with the insurance company, you want it to be on your timetable. You don't want to be pressured into a quick settlement by a doctor wanting his or her payment. There will be more details on this point later in the chapter.

2. Actual Wages Lost as a Result of the Accident

You should keep a log of all hours missed from your employment. Even if you use your sick or vacation time through your employer, you are still using an asset that would not be available to you for future use because of the accident. Therefore, you are entitled to have the auto insurance company reimburse you for lost wages. This should also include any time which your spouse lost from work on your behalf, as a result of the accident. In addition, keep a record of any benefits you lost as a result of being off work, such as sick and vacation time accumulation, employer contributions to your 401k and any other work related benefits.

3. Expenses for Mileage to and from the Doctor, Therapy, Trips to the Store, and Any Extra Miles Driven as a Result of the Accident

You should keep a log that lists the date of the trip, the purpose for the trip and of course, the miles driven. You should expect to be reimbursed at the same mileage rate the Internal Revenue Service uses for business miles driven. An example of this would be if you drove 350 miles as a result of the accident, you are entitled to receive 31 cents per mile, which amounts to $108.50 for the total miles driven. Also remember to include any tolls, parking fees and/or fares paid on public transportation.

4. Compensation for Temporary or Permanent Disability

This is a little tougher to determine, but not as complicated as you may think. Let's take a short-term disability as an example. You're involved in an accident and suffer a broken arm. In addition to any actual expenses incurred, you would be entitled to a monetary compensation for the broken arm. Most insurance companies use the same method in determining these amounts. Among other things, they use a chart that tells them what a reasonable settlement would be for a particular injury. The factors considered in determining these amounts are the severity of the injury, the age of the injured party and the possibility of partial or total disability. The older you are the more they may allow for an injury.

Normally you can get a good idea of how much they are willing to pay for a particular injury by their first offer and how they respond to your request for more. Most insurance companies will offer 10% to 20% below the maximum they are willing to pay, while others will offer you top dollar up front. No matter what their offer is, you should ask for 20% more. If they refuse immediately, wait a while, time is on your side. If after six to eight weeks they refuse to raise their offer, chances are they are offering the maximum they will pay. Another possibility is they may offer more than their initial amount, but not what you are asking for. This gives you a clue that there is potential for a higher settlement. ***Bear in mind, they may never give you the 20% more that you requested, but in the long run you will still come out a winner by personally negotiating with the insurance company.***

The insurance company has to obtain a medical release from each injured party in order to close their file. Usually the longer it takes, the more eager they are to settle the claim. Please realize this attitude may vary from company to company.

What about permanent or long-term disability? In the event of a permanent or long-term disability or fatality, you would usually get the policy's liability limits from the responsible party's liability insurance. In serious cases like this, the guess work is pretty well taken out of the process. ***If the "at fault" party has no insurance or their policy limits are not enough to cover the loss, you would then use the full limits on your uninsured and/or underinsured motorist coverages.*** In the case where a person has a minor permanent disability that doesn't affect their ability to work, etc., they may not recieve policy limits but would still be compensated for the disability.

As I've stated before, the insurance companies have a good idea of the dollar value of each disability. They know from experience and prior court cases the amount they can expect to pay for any given disability. They may bend some from this amount to avoid the high costs of going to court, but they won't write you a blank check either! I've seen many times when the insurance company will pay policy limits for a permanent disability that causes loss of income or physical mobility, etc. An all important question now arises, "How do I find out what the policy limits are of the ***"at fault"*** party?" We will answer this question later in this chapter.

5. Pain and Suffering

In addition to the actual expenses discussed above, you are also entitled to compensation for pain and suffering. A good rule of thumb for calculating pain and suffering is to take the total of actual medical expenses and multiply that number by 3. For example, if your medical expenses were $3,000, you would ask for $9,000, $3,000 of which were your actual expenses and $6,000 for your pain and suffering. This is a widely used formula and the insurance companies expect to pay this amount.

Once your bills are ready to submit to the insurance company, what next? ***The last thing you want to do is call an attorney! That's right, the last thing!*** Most insurance companies will be fair with you. Involving an attorney will only reduce your net settlement. The way to deal with the insurance company is to submit a well documented claim and ask for an amount well above what you expect to receive. In the case of serious injury, disability or a fatality, you would ask for a much larger amount. One million dollars or somewhere in that area is a good starting point. The reason you would ask for such a large amount is to find out if the ***"at fault"*** party carries a $1 million umbrella policy. When the insurance company makes an offer, you will have an idea of the responsible party's liability limit. At this point, they may even tell you they are offering policy limits, and if so, your work is done. You now know the maximum amount of coverage available to you. If they don't mention policy limits, you should ask for an itemization of their offer. In the itemization, you will see the limits allowed for disability, actual expenses, and pain and suffering. From this point, you can evaluate what areas, if any, you want to negotiate. An example would be if they offered X dollars for the injury, X dollars for actual expenses and X dollars for pain and suffering. You will know if the amount offered for pain and suffering is fair based on the 3 times medical formula. You would also know if the actual medical expenses are fair by comparing their offer to your actual medical expense list. From this point, you can then evaluate whether you want to ask for more. Usually you can get an additional 10% to settle just because the insurance company is more anxious to settle than you are. The leverage you have is the medical release form. The insurance company cannot close out your file until they have your signature on the release form. Be aware, many times an insurance company will push to have you sign the release form as soon as possible, offering you what appears to be a good settlement, but in reality the insurance company will be settling for as little as possible. My advice to you is refuse the initial offer and wait until your medical treatments are over and you have fully recovered. This could be a matter of several months to several years. ***Remember, time is on your side but be sure to check with the state department of insurance to find out what the statute of limitations is in your state.*** You don't want to go beyond that time limit. In many states you have up to two years to settle, but research it for yourself.

The last thing you want to say in your negotiations is, "I'll get an attorney." They hear this all the time and it means nothing to them other than showing them that you are unsure of what you are doing! If the insurance company thinks you don't know what you are doing, your settlement amount might not be as high as it would have been had you not mentioned the idea of an attorney. ***Confidence is the name of the game. If the insurance company feels you know what you are doing, you***

are more likely to get what you want, within reason of course.

6. Avoiding the Attorney's Gold Mine

The question most often asked, "Do I need an attorney?" ***A simple answer, no! That is the case 95% of the time. If you do hire an attorney, do it as a last resort, not first thing!*** Remember, the attorney will get a sizeable portion of your net settlement. Even if the attorney gets more money out of the insurance company, which he or she probably will, your net payment will probably be less. On average, a small claim handled by an attorney will net you about $2,000 less than a non-attorney handled claim. ***You will have an even higher dollar loss on a larger dollar or policy limits claim!***

I don't know about where you live, but I know where I live if it wasn't for attorneys we would not have daytime television. It seems that just about every advertisement is for an attorney wanting to protect you from the crooked insurance companies. They brainwash the public into thinking the insurance companies will be unfair in settling their claim and therefore, need their services!

Many times I've seen someone retain an attorney before the insurance company even knows the accident occurred. The public fails to realize that the insurance company, in most cases, will be fair. You just need to give them an opportunity to respond to the situation. ***These ambulance chasing attorneys know this, but are looking out for a sure dollar that belongs to you. They want their 35% to 50% cut!*** I cannot emphasize this point enough! This is your money we are talking about, not the attorney's. ***They want a large percentage of it for doing nothing!*** In most cases where fault is clear, the attorney sends a letter to the insurance company informing them that they represent the injured party. Then they wait for you to settle and the attorney collects his or her check! They know from the beginning it's a slam-dunk deal, but they see easy money and go after it! ***They should be tarred and feathered for such behavior. In my opinion, it's the closest thing to legal theft!***

Here Are Some Common Scenarios

Your vehicle is rear-ended by another vehicle and you sustain some injuries.

This is a classic example of the other party being 100% at fault. You have two choices. Your first choice is to deal directly with the insurance company representing the party at fault. If they don't have bodily injury liability coverage, you would then deal with your own insurance company providing you carry uninsured motorist coverage. One scenario would be you negotiate a settlement with the insurance company for $5,000, which based on what we have discussed is a fair settlement. You get your $5,000 and you're on your way. Same scenario, but this time you choose to call an attorney immediately following the accident so your rights will not be violated! The law firm is able to increase the settlement to $7,000. The attorney, based on a 35% split, receives $2,310. Guess what? You are now left with a net settlement of $4,690 or a total of $310 less than you would have received without the help of an attorney! In this case everyone except the attorney loses. You have lost $310 and the insurance buying public also lost because the additional $2,000 paid over and above the $5,000 could have been saved had you handled the loss yourself! The $2,000 the attorney stuck in his or her pocket is recouped by the insurance company with the next rate adjustment. In cases like the one described above, it is a no brainer for the attorney. Why else would they advertise their willingness to come to your hospital room, or call us first, etc. Normally, they don't do anything for you that you couldn't do for yourself because it is a cut and dry case. Who needs them? ***Attorneys know if the insurance company talks to you first, you will quickly realize that most insurance companies will be fair and that you do not need an attorney, thereby cutting out the attorneys on the gravy train!***

This problem is becoming so widespread that I've even heard of tow truck drivers at the scene of an accident referring people to an attorney. In some cases, they have referred people to a chiropractor, who in turn will refer the person to a law firm that the chiropractor works with. It is amazing how people will listen to anyone who comes along and worse yet, do what they say! Is a tow truck driver sufficiently informed to advise you on medical or legal matters? In the example above, guess who gets a portion of your settlement? You got it; the tow truck driver, the chiropractor, and of course, the attorney! ***Think about it!***

The only time you may want to talk to an attorney is if the insurance company is being unfair, and that has to be "big time" unfair. Remember, the attorney will get 35% to 50% of your total settlement! Don't call an attorney over a dispute in your settlement if it's a small dollar amount, or if it's out of pride or principle. It can cost you big dollars for that luxury! ***Remember, attorneys are to be used sparingly and as a last resort!***

What I Call the "Attorneys' Law"

Depending on where you live, you may encounter another scenario which indeed, may require an attorney. Some states have a law that may be referred to as contributory negligence. This law complicates the settlement process and therefore, increases the need for attorneys, hence, ***" the attorneys' law."*** This means both parties could share in the responsibility for the accident. The idea being that if it wasn't a clear cut situation and both drivers could have done something to avoid the accident but didn't, then they both would share in the responsibility for the accident.

An example of this would be a situation in which you are traveling down the road and as the light turns yellow, you decide to go through the intersection. Before you enter the intersection the light turns red, and as you pass through the intersection someone turns left in front of you and your vehicles collide. Who's at fault? You, because you ran the red light, or the other person for turning left in front of you? Based on the laws in most states, the person that turned left in front of you would be found at fault. But in states that have enacted the contributory negligence law, both of you are considered at fault. A percentage of fault would be assigned to each driver. Maybe 70% to the driver that turned left and 30% to the driver that ran the red light.

The legal profession has lobbied to have a considerable number of these laws enacted to confuse the issues and create a need for their services. The insurance companies have excellent legal departments and can determine the percentage of fault assigned to each driver, thereby reducing the need for an attorney in most situations.

7. Settling Uninsured and Underinsured Motorist Claims

The procedures for settling uninsured and underinsured motorist claims against your own insurance company are handled in the same manner as outlined above. The fact that you are dealing with your own insurance company doesn't matter, the procedure is the same.

8. How to Settle Property Damage, Collision and Comprehensive Losses

Property damage, as discussed in this chapter, will deal primarily with the repair of your vehicle. While property damage liability also covers buildings, fences, etc., it isn't my intention to discuss that area of the coverage at this time but to focus on the repair of the vehicle. The major issue in repairing the vehicle is getting the job done right. Hopefully, with the information provided in this portion of the chapter, you will have the tools necessary to do just that, and in addition ensure that your settlement with the insurance company is fair. These rules apply whether you are claiming under the other party's property damage liability or under your collision or comprehensive coverage.

Getting the Job Done Right

When your vehicle has been damaged, you want the repairs to be done correctly and the vehicle repaired to its condition prior to the accident. The first thing you want to do is locate a good repair shop to do the work. If you don't know of a good shop, the best way to find one is through your insurance company's claims department. Most companies will have a list of approved shops that meet their requirements for repair and service. Your first thought might be that the shop is only looking out for the interest of the insurance company. In most cases that isn't true, in fact, it is quite the opposite. The shop receives a great deal of business from the insurance company and therefore, is interested in doing a good job. If they didn't repair your vehicle satisfactorily, the insurance company would no longer use their services and the shop would lose a great deal of business. Many insurance companies, as well as the repair shops, will guarantee their work if it's done by a shop on the insurance company's approved list. In conclusion, using the insurance company's approved shops will generally give you the best repair and service possible. However, choosing a repair shop is your decision.

If there is a repair shop you want to use other than those on the approved list, you have the freedom to do so. A problem you may encounter is if the work is of poor quality, you would not have the insurance company's backing to ensure that the work is done to your satisfaction. Remember, it isn't the insurance company's responsibility to repair the vehicle, but only to compensate you for the damage. Several times, on behalf of a customer, I've contacted a shop on the approved list and told them if the repair wasn't done right I would notify the insurance company requesting the shop be removed from the approved list. You would be surprised how fast things got resolved! If the shop had not been on our approved list, there would have been nothing I could do to help.

Another question frequently asked is, ***"Why is it when you go into a repair shop they immediately ask if it is an insurance claim or are you paying for the repairs yourself?" If it's an insurance claim the price is usually higher.*** You would think it shouldn't make a difference, but it does. This is another example of how you and I, the insurance consumer, are being taken advantage of by the insurance industry. It is my opinion that the insurance industry is to blame because they tolerate, and even in some cases, encourage such activity. In the case of a small claim, you can get your compensation from the insurance company and then get the work done for less than if you had told the repair shop it was an insurance claim. The savings realized by doing this is yours to keep. If the insurance company wants to overpay you, that's their problem!

If you shop for the work that needs to be done, you will find a substantial spread between the estimates received from the various repair shops. These estimates could vary by as much as 30%. What you must do is ask what methods of repair your estimate is based on. This is the only way to measure which shop is really the best deal! Examples of the different repair methods would be: the sheet metal could be replaced or filled, or the paint could be applied only to the damaged area or to the entire side or section of the vehicle. These issues are very important! You want the painted area to match because in time it may fade, and you don't want fading on spots that are obvious thereby revealing the damaged area. Are they using new or salvaged parts? If they use new parts, are they factory parts or "after market" parts? These are some of the issues you will face in getting the vehicle repaired. If all things are equal, the price of the repair should be fairly close from shop to shop.

Whether you choose a shop based on the insurance company's approved list, or a shop of your preference, the above rules apply! In all my years of experience, there are only a few shops that I can recommend without hesitation because I know they will do the job right. ***Keep in mind not all repair shops are created equal!***

Total Loss Vs. Repairing the Vehicle

You may run into a situation where your vehicle appears to be a total loss, but the insurance company wants to repair it. The basic premise for repairing the vehicle is the value of the vehicle versus the cost of repair. If the cost to repair the vehicle is less than the value of the vehicle, they will repair it. If the cost of repair is more than the value of the vehicle, they will total it!

Many times I've heard people say, ***"I don't want the vehicle repaired, it will never be the same."*** They might be right, but the insurance company isn't concerned about that. They are looking strictly at the value of the vehicle versus the cost of repair. You may wish to sell the car after it's repaired, and that's your decision, but many times it can be the wrong decision if the repairs were done correctly. ***A good shop can repair a vehicle to be of better quality than originally built by the factory!***

Most insurance companies authorize the use of salvaged or after market parts. If this is of concern to you, check with the prospective insurance company before you purchase the policy. You may have a hard time finding an insurance company that doesn't use these kinds of parts. In my way of thinking, it's really not a problem if the part isn't a wear part such as an axle on a four wheel drive or some other part that can wear out. Sheet metal salvage is preferred over after market parts because you are getting factory parts that meet factory specifications, even though the parts are used. What is meant by sheet metal salvage is a door, fender, quarter panel, etc., from a wrecked vehicle. The only exception to this would be if the part came from an area of the country that has rust problems, in which case I would be concerned.

You may also find yourself in a situation where your vehicle has been damaged; however, it is an older vehicle and in excellent driving condition. You are still entitled to be compensated for the damage even if you decide not to fix the vehicle and put the money in your pocket instead.

An example would work this way: You have a vehicle worth $3,000 and it is damaged in such a way that it doesn't affect its safety or the way it drives. The damage is estimated at $1,500. It doesn't take much to do that amount of damage at today's repair costs. If you plan to drive the vehicle for several years, you may want to save the insurance money and apply it to your next vehicle purchase. If you drive that vehicle until it's about worn out, that $1,500 damage won't make a great deal of difference in the price when you sell it. I've seen many times when an insurance company totaled a vehicle that could be driven safely. If you desire, you can always purchase your vehicle back from the insurance company for salvage value. For example, the vehicle was worth $3,000 and you had a $500 deductible. Your final numbers would look like this. The value of the vehicle is $3,000 minus the $500 deductible minus the salvage value of $300, leaving you with a settlement of $2,200 and your damaged vehicle. You have the option of doing this when you settle on a total loss, regardless of the value of the vehicle.

Most insurance policies covering collision and comprehensive are written on an actual cash value at time of loss basis. On new vehicle leases or purchases, you can usually buy new for old replacement coverage that will replace your vehicle with a new one of like make and model, rather than allowing used value for the vehicle. Of course, there is an additional cost for the coverage, but well worth it if you don't want to take the risk of being ***"upside down"*** on your loan or lease. Being ***"upside down"*** means that the vehicle was a total loss and you owe more on the loan or lease than the vehicle was worth. This is a common occurrence in the first three to four years after one purchases or leases a new vehicle.

If you don't have replacement cost coverage on your vehicle and it is a total loss, the compensation will be actual cash value at time of loss. If you don't think it's a fair settlement, ask them to supply documentation showing how they arrived at the settlement amount. If you're unhappy with their explanation, ask where you could purchase a comparable vehicle for the settlement amount offered plus your deductible. If they are unable to supply you with that information, you could do some shopping on your own and present your findings to the insurance company. It's a bit of work, but in my opinion well worth the extra effort. Usually it will increase your settlement to a fair amount!

I am confident that the information in this chapter will be of benefit to you in the event of a claim, whether it's against your own insurance company or the company of another motorist responsible for causing the accident. ***Hopefully, you will never have to use the information in this chapter, but if you do, it will prove invaluable!***

Chapter 5

Preparing for the 21st Century

Chapter 5

Preparing for the 21st Century

1. The Winds of Change

Change in the insurance industry is happening so fast that by the time you read this book, some of what I've written regarding upcoming changes will be old news!

We live in an age of constant change. Who would have thought a few years ago we would be making our own investment transactions with the help of home computers. Think of the commission savings involved by making these transactions yourself. Through computers, we now have the ability to do our banking from home, print checks, and/or have the bank transfer money directly from our accounts, never having to lick a stamp! Every time you turn around, the bank or brokerage industry is offering a new service or discount you can take advantage of on your home computer.

Through the use of the Internet, we have the ability to purchase all kinds of goods and services without leaving our home or having to deal with pushy sales people. We can even shop from our television 24 hours a day. Have you ever bought anything that way?

What stops us from buying our auto insurance without the help of an agent? Nothing that I know of except the insurance industry's slow response to change and the public's lack of knowledge and desire. At the present time, you can buy auto insurance in Canada through the Internet. In the United States there are several major insurance companies that have web sites, although most of them are public relations spots. While marginally useful, they're really not of much value. Some services on the Internet allow you to get quotes from several different insurance companies for life and auto insurance. I just read recently where a major insurance company is offering auto insurance purchases via the Internet. ***It's about time!*** As I've said before, the technology is there but the insurance buying public and the insurance industry, by and large, are not ready for the change. The purpose for this book is to inform you of the possibilities, prepare you for the change, educate and encourage you to demand the availability of buying your auto insurance without a commissioned agent. ***Whether you use the Internet or an 800 number dealing directly with a customer service representative, the savings can be substantial!***

2. The Insurance Company of the Future

The insurance company of the future will appear far different than it is today. You will still be dealing with an insurance company, but you will be able to purchase the policy from a bank, a credit union, an insurance agent, the Internet, an 800 number, or ways not yet thought of. In the future, there will be fewer insurance companies to select from because many are merging in order to reduce their costs. The true profit margin is so small and competition so fierce, that companies who fail to reduce their costs will not survive. The insurance industry is frantically trying to stay ahead of the technology curve. Technology is here for providing more efficient and cost effective methods of sales and services, but the application of such is the missing factor. It's not uncommon for insurance companies to be so stressed over this issue that they make hasty changes in their policy service procedures, trying to get ahead of the curve. Even though their programs often do not work properly when first introduced, they continue to use them, running the risk of losing a few customers. These hasty changes result in numerous errors and confusion, not only for the agency force, but for the customer as well. As a result of the confusion, the confidence of the customer has been shaken; therefore, many good accounts have taken their business to other insurance companies.

This certainly underscores the frantic pace of change, and the insurance industry's overall inability to keep up with it. They are literally tripping over themselves to deliver the best possible service at the lowest possible price. ***It's like turning a battleship around in a bathtub, an impossible task without major modifications!***

Another fly in the ointment; foreign companies are entering the U.S. market and purchasing insurance companies. Two major U.S. insurance companies have been purchased by foreign companies; one by a British company, the other by a French company. Change is so rapid in the industry that by the time you read this, there will probably be additional foreign involvement. These foreign companies, as well as the American companies, are looking to make as much profit as possible, which is the American way. ***Their concern isn't for your well being, but strictly profit!***

As stated earlier, the insurance companies are not keeping up with the rapid pace of technology changes required to remain competitive. They are reducing regional office staff and shifting more of their workload to the agency force. This is an attempt to lower their expense ratio to compete with the newer and smarter companies who are advancing into the 21st Century, and are not encumbered by outdated systems and agent contracts. These smart companies are fairly new companies, or older companies which have been revitalized by another company who has money and a vision for the future. Some of the older companies in the industry have avoided the mistakes of their competitors and have a low overhead operation and therefore, need less reshaping. In either case, new or revitalized, these companies will beat the major companies that cannot change quickly. Most major companies have so much overhead built into their systems that restructuring would be almost impossible without substantial customer loss. The smarter companies have eliminated the agency force, cut overhead to the bone, and are approximately 15% to 20% cheaper for comparable coverages, and still able to give an acceptable level of service. If the company has had a recent infusion of cash from an experienced insurance company, and has initiated operational changes, their past isn't necessarily a reflection of the future. This would be the only exception involving a company that isn't rated an "A" by A.M. Best, and a company that you should strongly consider. This information is available from A.M. Best, Standard and Poors, or other related reference materials found at the public library.

Let me explain how you can act as your own agent by telling you what the agent actually does. When you contact an agent's office for a quote, they go directly to their computer and rate the auto, homeowner's or other type of coverage requested with the information you have supplied them. Once the policy has been rated, they call, mail or fax the information to you. If you want to have the agent write the policy, the agent goes back to the computer and enters the pertinent information. With most companies, if the information you gave the agent is correct, the policy will be issued and sent directly to you. Most agents never process the paper work associated with your policy.

Once you are their customer and you call with a claim or a change of any kind to your policy, they again enter the pertinent information into the computer. The information is then sent directly to the appropriate office or department and handled by the company. Normally, the agent doesn't have anything to do with adjusting your claim or providing any real service to your account that you couldn't do with the help of a home computer or an 800 number. The only service the agent may provide is information which I have made available to you in this book. ***My question is, "Why are you paying the agent anywhere from 7% to 20% of your insurance premium to do those things you can do yourself?"*** Is it the calendar, or birthday and/or Christmas card you receive that makes it worth the extra money? Get real! The agent's role is becoming a thing of the past just as the stock broker, bank teller and eventually, the car salesman. In the long run, the insurance agent will go the way of the buggy whip maker of 100 years ago. Chances are your grandchildren will grow up not knowing what an insurance agent is. Is it obvious to you now that you are paying a considerable sum of money for unnecessary hand holding? ***My advice is save the money and do it yourself!***

In the future, insurance companies will be more selective as to who they insure. They can now obtain more information about an individual and faster than ever before. You will see approximately 20% to 30% of the insurance buyers getting the ultra preferred rates and everyone else getting a blend of standard and substandard rates. To qualify for the ultra preferred rates, you may have to be accident and citation free, insured with a preferred company for at least two to five years, be claim free, and have "near perfect" credit. Customer selection is becoming a science with everyone trying to get the edge on their competition. The ideal insurance customer is one who pays their premium on time and never has a loss. That may sound impossible but I have had customers for 10 to 20 years and have never had a single loss! This type of customer is what all insurance companies are looking for.

3. The Agent of the Future

If you are young and just starting out in the insurance business, you may want to consider another field of endeavor. The role of the agent and the agency operation is changing rapidly. In the past, the insurance agent was viewed as a friend you trusted with your insurance affairs. You could call or drop in at their office and get your business taken care of, leaving with the confidence that you received personal attention. You believed your agent was honest with you and with the insurance company he or she represented and all was well.

Most agents are independent contractors paid on a commission basis. The majority of costs associated with running the agency are the agent's responsibility. Depending on the size of the agency, its location and the number of employees, the cost could be as little as $20,000 or as much as $75,000 or higher per year! The agency has to sell a lot of policies just to cover the overhead. It's true that the lion's share of the income is from renewals, but the fact remains, new policies are vitally important to the agency. With competition from other companies, customers moving away, dying, or for whatever reason their policy goes out of force, the average agency experiences 8% to 15% policy turnover per year. Some agencies that write standard business can experience turnover as high as 60% or more per year. The bottom line is the agency has to produce a fair amount of new customers to stay afloat. Added to that is pressure from the insurance company to meet sales quotas. The end result is an unhealthy situation for both the insurance company and the insurance consumer.

The insurance companies, in order to reduce their expense ratio, have shifted more of the overhead to the agency force without increasing commissions to offset the additional workload. One major insurance company recently cut agents' commissions by approximately 33%, while expecting the agents to take on more of the duties which the company handled in the past. Another major insurance company is in the process of changing their agents' agreements from an employee status to contractor status. This change will allow the company to shift more of its work, with no corresponding pay raise, to the agent and eventually make it easier to eliminate the agency force altogether when the insurance company is ready to do so. You now have an agency force that doesn't have time to give the personal service which you expect and have grown accustomed to.

The agents, in order to meet quotas or just stay afloat, have to do whatever they can to write the policies needed. Agents are now doing more of the company's main office work, e.g., underwriting and policy service. Therefore, they don't have to be as careful when it comes to customer selection as they have in the past. The company isn't looking over the agent's shoulder as in the past, nor does the agent have to tell the company everything the customer tells him or her. The agent can give you a lower rate than you're entitled to in order to sell you the policy. It has become common practice among agents to misrepresent information to the insurance company, knowing they will not be detected. This is a direct result of the insurance companies' efforts to cut costs, thereby, leaving no one to catch the misrepresentation of facts. As a result, the commissioned agent makes the sale at a premium amount less than what is fair. ***Unfortunately you and I, the honest customers, are subsidizing the rate structure by paying more than our fair share in premiums in order to make up for the dishonest agents!*** This kind of activity is more prevalent than you would like to think and has been increasing in recent years. You could shop the same insurance company with several agents using the same vehicles, coverages, drivers, etc., and get several different quotes. It doesn't take long to find an agent that is hungry for business and willing to misrepresent for you. Occasionally, the insurance company finds out about this kind of activity and one of two things will happen. Either the agent will be reprimanded for his or her actions and threatened with termination or the most common response being nothing happens at all! In fact, some district and regional managers encourage such activity if it can be done discreetly. There are many ways to manipulate the rules or to flat out misrepresent, that even the company cannot detect. You must remember that district and regional managers are, for the most part, commissioned sales people and have quotas to meet just as the agent does! The overall tendency is to look out for the short-term which is their job, and disregard the future and financial health of the insurance company, as well as the interest of the consumer. Many companies will overlook such activity if the agent involved is a big producer, especially if the production is in life insurance. They don't want to affect the forward momentum of the agent or blemish his or her record. At this point, I must say this activity isn't what the higher levels of management desire. In most cases, it's more of a regional management problem and may vary from place to place and company to company around the country. Depending on who is in charge of that particular region, this kind of activity will either flourish or be discouraged.

The real disadvantage to the honest insurance consumer is their premiums are higher than they should be because they are paying a portion of someone else's premium. An example of this would be you drive 12 miles one way to work but the agent misrepresents and says you drive 8 miles one way to work. The policy will cost about 10% less than if it had been rated correctly. The 10% that you didn't pay will have to be shared by all insurance consumers. Multiply that example by thousands and you get an idea of the magnitude of the problem that you and I are paying for! Think of it as every time you purchase an item in the store, the cost of that item includes an amount to cover shoplifting. The same principle applies here but in this example the store, which is the insurance company, is encouraging the theft and adding it on to your premium costs! It's as if a major retailer encourages theft so they can meet sales quotas and add the cost of the theft to the retail price! This is just one example of the many ways misrepresentation occurs. ***The insurance industry will not admit that they permit this kind of activity, but they do!***

The problem has gotten out of hand, and with the agents having more authority on how policies are written, more automation and fewer people looking over their shoulders, it's like an open checkbook to the agent. This is just one more reason to avoid insurance companies that have a commissioned sales force. Not only will you remove a layer of expense but also eliminate paying for the misrepresentation that goes on within the company by its own agents.

In the future, there will be fewer agents but their agencies will be larger. The marginal agencies will not be able to handle the additional overhead due to the additional workload and therefore, will sell out and leave the business altogether or work as an employee for a larger agency. This is already happening. ***It will be like dealing with a small insurance company rather than an agent.*** You will deal with an employee of the agency and not the agent. The agent will become the office manager. The agency will also do in-house underwriting and eventually adjust claims. Some insurance companies already have their agents adjusting small claims. Since you won't be dealing directly with the agent but an office staff member, why not cut that level of expense out altogether and deal directly with the insurance company? You won't experience the personal service of the past either way you go!

You may be asking the questions, ***"Why don't insurance companies eliminate agents altogether and why are they trying to maintain the old system?"*** The answer is one or more of three basic reasons that follow.

The first reason is some of the larger insurance companies are unwilling to admit that they need to change in order to survive, or they recognize the need for change but are unable to adapt.

The second reason, and probably a more valid one, is they are in a real bind. They don't have the technology in place to eliminate the agency force just yet and therefore, are keeping them during the transition. When the transition is complete and all is working smoothly, the agency force will be out the door. In my opinion, that's the situation with many of the larger companies. They may say they are committed to the agency force, but in reality they are automating in such a way that the groundwork is being laid for an agentless operation. They don't want to, nor can they afford to, let the agents go until they are sure the agents are no longer needed. They have too much at stake to let them go before the systems are up and running flawlessly. Once the larger companies succeed at eliminating the agency force, the smaller companies will follow suit in order to compete and survive. I personally don't believe that these companies want to delete their agency force for the sake of doing so, but I believe they are being forced to by the changes in the insurance industry.

The third reason is found in two words, ***"life insurance."*** It isn't my intention at this time to go into great detail on this subject, so I will limit my comments to the following. Life insurance is a product that guarantees a profit for the insurance company. All insurance companies use the same mortality tables and can predict the amount of profit they will make. With that as a basis, you must realize that all things being equal, all life insurance products should be priced the same if the products were structured the same. This is where the smoke and mirrors come into play. You can get quotes on two identical life products from two different life insurance companies and find the rates to be very different. The reasons can be many but here are the foundational ones.

First, you have the agent's commission which can range from 50% to 110% or higher of the first year's premium, then a reduced commission beyond that time period. You can, in most cases, buy life insurance without an agent and save anywhere from to 20% to 40% or more over the long term! The next reason is the auto insurance company knows that you, the loyal customer, will in most cases, buy life insurance from your auto or homeowner's insurance agent without shopping other life products. Therefore, they not only price the products high for the maximum profit margin, but they are slow to offer new products that the industry is moving towards. They don't see a need to change their life products until sales of current products slow, and then act like they just invented the new products and are kind enough to offer them to you. When in reality, the only reason it's offered at all is because sales have slowed on the old products and they are losing existing policies to companies offering the new products. You, the customer, is unaware of what is really taking place because you trust your agent and the insurance company. It happens all the time! A customer calls up and wants X dollars of life insurance and wants to purchase it from their property and casualty agent. The agent knows the product is overpriced, but because he or she has contracted to sell the company's products, the agent cannot say anything, let alone recommend another company's product. It's sad that people who are so trusting are being taken advantage of.

Have you ever had your auto or homeowner's insurance agent sell you a life insurance product and several years later come to you with a better product to replace the old one? Have you ever asked yourself why he or she didn't sell you the better product originally? Was it because the insurance company just came out with the new product? ***The real question to ask is, "Why has this process happened to me more than once?" My advice to you is never buy life insurance from an agent that sells auto and homeowner's insurance. You will be paying far too much!***

You have no idea how hard the companies push for life sales! If I had a dollar for every time we had a life insurance contest or for every flier that the company put out pushing life sales, I would be wealthy. It is my personal opinion that if casualty insurance companies didn't sell life insurance, it would be another reason to eliminate the agents altogether. Look at the casualty companies that don't have agents. Many of them don't sell life insurance, and the ones that do, sell at a much lower rate.

One final word on life insurance, no matter who you buy life insurance from, it's my belief that you need to buy only the coverage necessary for final expenses and to replace lost income for your family, not for investment purposes. Just as in auto insurance, buying life insurance is the same without an agent, only a simpler product to understand. If you would like a more in-depth study on the subject of purchasing life insurance, please see the offer in the back of this book featuring, ***"The Great Life Insurance Hoax."***

In summing up this portion of the chapter, I trust I have made it clear that an agent can be an expensive luxury. Without one you will reduce costs substantially, and possibly experience only a minor loss in service as far as personal attention is concerned. In some cases, depending on the quality of your agent now, the service might be better. In addition, you will have access to 24-hour insurance service centers or Internet access. ***Once you get accustomed to the idea of not having an agent and learn a few basics, you will be on your way to big savings!***

4. The Insurance Consumer of the Future

The insurance consumer of the future will be well educated, computer literate and able to think for themselves in making decisions relating to their insurance needs. The basics of insurance are very simple and once learned, will serve you well into the future.

The older generation who insists on personal service will, in time, retire from the scene. The younger generation of latchkey kids who were brought up on television and computers have not experienced personal interaction with others like the older generation. As a result, they have had to be more self-sufficient. They will be perfectly content to do business on an impersonal basis. In fact, it is my belief they will prefer that approach rather than dealing with people. They will also be a less loyal group of customers and the issue of personal service will be of minor concern to them. It will seem perfectly normal for them to sit down at their computer, search for the best deal and change to another company, even for minor savings. I'm not saying that's bad, but I do believe it is the direction in which the insurance industry is headed.

The insurance buyer of the future will be able to purchase insurance on their home computer, transfer funds to pay for the insurance, file claims and even communicate with the company through e-mail regarding policy service or any questions they might have.

The insurance buyer of the future can help bring these changes about by contacting their insurance company and demanding they be allowed to deal directly with the insurance company and save the agent overhead. Call, or better yet, write your insurance company and insist that they make available the means to deal directly with them or you will shop for a company which will. You will be surprised at how fast the industry will respond to these requests!

Discounts available from most auto insurance companies.

Don't neglect to ask about these or any other discounts offered!

Multi-car - two or more cars in household (not necessarily garaged at the same location).

Auto-home - insuring your home, apartment or condominium with the same company you insure your vehicle with.

Multi-policy - having other policies such as life insurance with the same company.

Good student - students with a specified grade average.

Age - for senior citizens or other age categories, sometimes starting as young as 25.

Retirees - based on reduced miles driven because of retirement.

Driver's education or safety certification classes - regardless of driver's age.

Anti-lock brakes

Airbag or passive restraint devices

Anti-theft devices - such as car alarms

Longevity - insuring with the same insurance company over a period of several years.

Claim free history - often given as a premium reduction or a reduction of your deductible in the event of a claim.

NOTE: This list is by no means conclusive, but should cover most discounts offered by insurance companies.

The $aving$ Calculator

Current Coverage		Proposed Coverage	
Bodily Injury Liability ____________	Premium _______	Coverage __________	Premium _______
Property Damage ______________	Premium _______	Coverage __________	Premium _______
Uninsured Motorist _____________	Premium _______	Coverage __________	Premium _______
Underinsured Motorist ___________	Premium _______	Coverage __________	Premium _______
Medical/PIP __________________	Premium _______	Coverage __________	Premium _______
Collision Deductible ____________	Premium _______	Coverage __________	Premium _______
Comprehensive Deductible ______	Premium _______	Coverage __________	Premium _______
Towing ______________________	Premium _______	Coverage __________	Premium _______
Car Rental ___________________	Premium _______	Coverage __________	Premium _______
Miscellaneous Coverage ________	Premium _______	Coverage __________	Premium _______

Current Total Premium $____________ **Proposed Premium $_____________**

Savings $____________

Copy This Sheet to Use for Your Shopping Convenience

Afterword

If you follow the information in this book, you will easily save 25% plus on your auto insurance. It has been my goal to give you a guide which is easy to read and understand that not only teaches you how to save money on your auto insurance, but also how to handle claims, select proper coverages, select the right insurance company, resolve problems and many other areas of concern that arise.

It has taken every spare minute for the last 11 months to accomplish the task of completing this book. To my knowledge, it is accurate and complete.

If you find any areas you do not understand or that haven't been addressed or made clear, I would like to hear from you. I plan to revise and update this book periodically and feel that your input would be invaluable for future editions. I would also like to hear about your experiences and savings enjoyed by applying the principles outlined in this book. Please write to: Alan Abler c/o Heidi House LTD, 18631 N. 19th Avenue, Suite #128-222, Dept C, Phoenix, AZ 85027. ***Your input would be greatly appreciated!***

More Valuable Information You Can't Afford to Miss!!

Book 1

How to $ave 25% Plu$ on Your Homeowner'$ In$urance

1. Understanding Your Policy (it's simple)
2. Selecting the Best Policy For You
3. How to Settle a Claim to Your Benefit
4. How to Avoid Losses (saving you big dollars)
5. Selecting the Right Insurance Company
6. Plus Many Other Money Saving Tips

Book 2

The Great Life Insurance Hoax

1. Buy Only the Coverage You Need (don't over buy)
2. Where to Get the Best Coverage for the Price
3. Who to Avoid When Purchasing Your Life Insurance
4. How to Separate Life Insurance from Investments
5. Learn the Three Great Myths the Life Insurance Industry Uses
6. The Smart Way to Plan for Retirement

These Valuable Guides Can Be Yours for $9.95 Each Including Shipping and Handling — Or Save by Ordering Both for the Incredibly Low Price of $14.95 which includes First Class Shipping and Handling

To order copies of these books, fill out this form or call today.
Please send the books I've marked to:

Name ____

Address ______________________________ Apt ________

City ____________________ State ____________ Zip ________

Book Title	Cost Ea.	Quantity	Total
How to $ave 25% Plu$ on Your Homeowner's In$urance	**$ 9.95**		
The Great Life Insurance Hoax	**$ 9.95**		
Combo package of both books	**$ 14.95**		
	Subtotal		
	Arizona residents add 7.05% Sales Tax		
	TOTAL		

For Credit Card Orders Please Complete:

Visa ___MasterCard___ AMEX___ Card Number ____________________

Expiration_______ Signature ______________________________

Mail This Order Form to: **Heidi House LTD**
18631 N. 19th Avenue, Suite #128-222
Phoenix, AZ 85027

Phone orders 1-888-511-6070 for prompt delivery! ***Have your credit card ready!***
Or Fax orders to 1-602-780-1704.

Please allow 2 to 4 weeks for delivery.